UNLEASH

DISCOVER THE KEY TO MONETIZING

YOUR

YOUR OWN PERSONAL BRAND

BRAND

TONY D'ONOFRIO

UNLEASH YOUR BRAND

DISCOVER THE KEY TO MONETIZING
YOUR OWN PERSONAL BRAND

TONY D'ONOFRIO

TONY D'ONOFRIO INSIGHTS
TONYDONOFRIO.COM

FOREWORD

BY ROBERT LOCKE

A SEASONED ENTERPRISE EXECUTIVE AND FORMER STARTUP CEO.
HIGHLY RESPECTED WITHIN FORTUNE 100 COMPANIES, SILICON VALLEY
STARTUPS AND THE VENTURE CAPITAL COMMUNITY.

I've known Tony since 2008 and since then have had a front row seat to the events and actions described in this book. *Unleash Your Brand* is an inspirational story of redemption and a good man overcoming the obstacles between him and his rightful place in the world. It is also an instructional manual which guides the reader, showing how to apply the same lessons Tony has learned in order to achieve the kind of success and freedom that he has earned.

I watched Tony navigate the treacherous corporate waters. I watched him put together the plan that he shares in this book. And I watched him execute that plan and succeed at an extraordinary level. The most remarkable thing about his journey is the fact that Tony didn't reinvent himself. He simply used the tools available to share with the world who he is and what he knows, and the world embraced him.

I've called Tony countless times over the years to ask him to reveal his story and insights so that people I have been helping could benefit from what he has learned and I'm delighted that his wisdom and knowledge are now available to everyone. Tony has created his own brand, his own future. He wants the same for you. By investing the time to read *Unleash Your Brand*, you have that opportunity.

INTRODUCTION

Ten years ago, I encountered a career setback. At what I anticipated would be a personal celebratory dinner, the major promotion I had been craving was awarded to someone else.

The long, sleep deprived hours that followed became a tipping point to reset and redefine the direction of my career, my life. Rather than relying on the corporate ladder and eventually reaching a successful retirement age, instead I began to craft a brand that would showcase my personal value. On a hotel napkin (how I wish I had kept it!), I started scribbling ideas. What instruments around me were available to tell my story? How could I build a brand capable of instantly changing careers? What legacy did I want to leave my children? How could I design a persona and create a life journey devoid of regrets?

Devastating as it was, that evening prompted me to recraft my destiny. Since then, across multiple platforms, I have been named as a top 100 global retail influencer. Over 150,000 people follow my content on LinkedIn while surpassing 10,000 direct contacts; my YouTube channel is growing, and I continue to write about innovation, retail and leadership. All because I have built my own memorable and unique brand by breaking the chains that originally confined me.

My lightbulb moment was the realization that, all around us, technology was changing the definition of individual value. During the intervening years, vivid details of my sleepless night at

Heathrow's Marriott Hotel continued to reverberate in my mind. Hours of reflective thinking led to a major reassessment of long-term professional goals. Which is why my passion for innovation that began while in my first post university employment gradually evolved into my *Disruptive Future of Retail*, a presentation I have continuously updated. What started out as a simple industry update to retailers, eventually transitioned into my unique, inspiring innovation message to audiences on many global stages, forecasting the future of the vibrant retail industry.

The timing of my discovery of personal branding was perfect, given that this was when social media channels were aggressively growing around me. I quickly focused on LinkedIn as a B2B platform for engagement. In fact, LinkedIn contacted me and we have mutually assisted each other to expand the content.

Meanwhile, I also realized that someday I would retire and would need something creative to keep me busy. What I did not, at the time, appreciate was that personal branding would actually accelerate my next career move.

The reason I retired 10 years early from my corporate career was because my personal brand took off. Turns out my focus on innovation and leadership had a positive linkage with fast growing technology companies and startups in Silicon Valley. I 'retired' from corporate life one Friday; the following Tuesday (yes, only a long weekend of rest), I was at my first Board of Directors meeting with a leading technology company. Pre-pandemic, twice a year, I would trek to Silicon Valley to meet with 25 global startups to decide which to advise or invest in to their next level.

Multiple other board assignments in both the US and Europe followed, all while my personal brand experienced growing success. Those board assignments opened up other opportunities. As an example, a couple of advisory board positions at one company led to a two-year assignment to run their global retail security business. In those short two years, using innovation lessons from Silicon Valley,

I was successfully reinventing the future of retail loss prevention. In August 2023 I took on my biggest corporate role to date, President for a major division of a Fortune 500 company.

For TD Insights, which is my personal branding company, my greatest passion is to continuously explore opportunities to engage my audience with new ideas for mutual improvement. This includes constant research on trends and innovation, a live YouTube channel, a personal website, and lots of personal articles that are re-published on other platforms.

As you will learn in this book, there are multiple techniques available that allow you to multi-task between corporate and personal branding activities. As you monetize your personal brand, you can hire individuals to assist in continuing to increase its value.

Because a successful personal brand requires focus, your skills to prioritize will increase. You will also attract talented individuals that will allow you to do more with less. As I took on the role of President of that Fortune 500 division, with a social media manager and a professional publicist, we re-prioritized current personal branding activities at TD Insights to those that have the highest long-term value and they will continue with my periodic, less frequent input.

The key driver of my brand success has been my laser focus on win-win customer relationships. I was fortunate, because of my senior executive roles, to be able to engage with retailers on a global scale. On every continent, I built lasting partnerships whose fruits I am still enjoying today as lifetime friendships.

But there is no smooth road; all of us encounter life challenges in our journey through time. For me personally, arriving in a big US city from a small town in the mountains of Italy at the age of 11 was a major cultural shock. Not getting the promotion I really wanted was a gut-wrenching setback. Feeling as if you are constantly on stage can be frightening. Navigating and optimizing messaging can feel like a thankless time-consuming task. But setbacks can either be moments when you give up or opportunities to analyze their message before resetting to the next goal. In other words, obstacles define who you become.

The American Dream is alive in each of us. How we wake up to its reality is *totally* under our control. You must truly believe that if you dream it, provided you work hard enough, and don't let setbacks stop you, you will craft an amazing life for yourself and also inspire future generations to greater success.

So, if you are in a career rut, unsure what next step to take, this is your book. If you are already climbing that endless corporate ladder, I can confirm that you are at risk by not applying the lessons explained in subsequent chapters. If you are an introvert, fearing the persona you are holding within, read on. If you are extrovert, your cockiness is your best asset that can be fine-tuned through a personal branding formula to even greater success. If you are young, just like compound interest, you will multiply the lessons of personal branding to unbelievable possibilities. If you are middle aged or old, it's never too late to start. At every age, you can transform and upgrade your career and life to a new level because, whether you realize it or not, the personality you project to the world is your personal brand, a key aspect of your private and professional life. And that deserves – demands – investment.

Unleash Your Brand is my personal guide to enable you to recognize those distinctive character traits that will form the foundation of your own unique brand. In this book, I will explore the value of developing that brand while exploiting the opportunities it presents, as well as identifying branding channels and the process behind achieving and maintaining branding success. In essence, I will demonstrate the ongoing repercussions of breaking the chains of monotony and replacing predictable careers with life-changing personal branding which puts you in charge of your destiny.

I have built my successful brand. Now I want to help you discover and monetize *yours*.

CONTENTS

THE VALUE OF A PERSONAL BRAND

> **'YOUR BRAND IS WHAT PEOPLE SAY ABOUT YOU WHEN YOU ARE NOT IN THE ROOM.'**
>
> JEFF BEZOS

When was the last time you Googled your name? In a world with intensive communications, your personal brand is being defined either by others such as your company / friends or by you through channels such as social media.

Like it or not, you already have a personal brand and at any point in your life, you can take the initiative to control that brand and make it more valuable. In this first chapter we will explore why you need to take control of your personal branding, the risks with social media, reasons why you need a personal brand, and its importance for maximizing your long-term success. Because your best asset to stay ahead of the competition is, and always will be, how you project your values and capabilities via your personal brand.

A BRIEF HISTORY OF BRANDING

The modern word 'brand' is derived from the ancient Norse word 'brandr' meaning 'to burn.' In the 1300s, a brand described a torch or a burning piece of wood used as a tool. Two hundred years later, the meaning had evolved to a mark showing ownership. Fast forward to the 1820s and, with the introduction of mass production and increased trading, marking goods enabled traders to distinguish themselves from competitors.

As trademarks – first registered in the 1870s – prevented competitors from creating confusingly similar products, brands evolved into a symbol of quality rather than ownership. But it was in 1928 that Edward Bernays, nephew of Sigmund Freud, argued in his book, *Propaganda*, that by associating products with ideas, larger numbers of people could be convinced to change their behavior.[1] The New York Madison Avenue advertising crowd listened and by the 1960s marketers were using mass media to associate brands with emotional benefits, rather than functional ones.

During the 1980s, as products went global, companies shifted to increasing the value of the corporate or company brand. This allowed them to build stronger loyalty across extended product lines. In 1984 Apple broke the mould further with their iconic ad[2] on breaking free from rigid conformity which was prevalent in the computer industry. Post that Apple moment, companies more intensely focused on corporate identity versus short brand campaigns. As advertising agencies evolved into brand consultancies, in turn, corporate branding extended to non-profits, political groups and celebrities' personal brands.

The internet, mobile phones and social media are the foundational next generation technology elements available to enable us to become active brand consultants in building a personalized transformational future. Personal branding is the next logical step in the evolution of branding and the sooner you leverage this emerging megatrend, the more valuable your brand will become.

This is your Apple moment. It is time for you to trademark yourself as a differentiated valuable resource for both your company and the world around you by creating and nurturing your own unique personal brand.

WHAT IS PERSONAL BRANDING?

Personal branding is the deliberate crafting of your public persona including all published content created to shape it. This only works long term if it is crafted based on your particular skills and discovering how those skills add value to the world around you. Genuine self-expression, built on skills that are fine-tuned over time, is what builds successful personal brands. Fake brands fail, and fail substantially over time.

Building a personal brand is a process and never a single magical step. It must include a clear identity definition, differentiation versus competitors, and come across consistently as recognizable and relatable to an audience.

Do not get personal branding confused with your reputation. Perception and credibility are factors that, long term, build a reputation. However, personal branding is purposeful visibility of thought leadership ideas that extend your professional skills to a wider audience.

Are you one of those individuals working in a business that receives annual performance reviews? Think of the personal brand as the launch of Me.Inc. Instead of relying on a company to define you through those reviews, with a personal brand, you are taking control and, as it builds, actively marketing to a broader audience both within and outside your company the value of you as an individual.

Think of the liberating aspects of what you have just read. Instead of a company that has only known you for the time of employment defining your value, you are standing up professionally both internally and externally and eventually will command greater respect from your peers and customers through your personal brand.

Succinctly, the end result of a well-executed personal brand is greater autonomy. You, not your employer, are in control of your destiny. As in my career, new opportunities for growth emerge, putting the timetable for major life transition moments totally under your control.

Ambition and, more importantly, willingness to put in the work to deliver a differentiated value proposition of you as an individual are fundamental in building your personal brand. Your true value, both at a personal and professional level, will be elevated through the process of discovering your true self.

Because of technology, we have come a long way from the historical ancient Norse definition of a brand. And if you are reading this book, you already have that 'burning fire' in you to achieve something special in your life.

A strategically well-executed personal brand will:

o   Turn your name into a monetizable asset
o   Find you a valuable value-sharing global audience
o   Create multiple alternative paths to success
o   Increase trust and credibility
o   Lead to more curiosity and invaluable continuous learning
o   Allow you to take control of your online narrative
o   Increase top-of-mind awareness
o   Leave a lasting positive legacy

Let's now go into the details of each of these important reasons to create and nurture a personal brand.

Turn Your Name into a Valuable Monetizable Asset

You are unique. Your family life, education, work experiences, social engagements and much more have crafted your special personality. All of us at various times of our lives have wished for greater aspirations in what we ultimately want to accomplish. Dreaming and actually committing to taking action to achieve your goals are oceans apart.

But when it comes to something as simple as your name, how unique are we really in this big wide world? When I Google my name, the search engine delivers nearly 2 million results in less than a second.

Surprisingly, when I enter my name on Linkedin, 15 pages of individuals with the same name emerge.

A personal brand, over time, will elevate the importance and value of YOU as an individual. Today, my name consistently appears as number one in the Google search engine. I am not bragging. I am simply stating that the work put into building a personal brand has reaped rewards in name recognition.

Name recognition delivers expanded opportunities for personal and professional growth. It gives you freedom to explore alternative roads to take your future. Instead of worrying what I am going to do next, it automatically puts more irons in the fire for you to consider.

Exploit a Valuable Value-Sharing Global Audience

In global presentations, I have shared that the retail industry has been transformed by three major megatrends post World War II. Prior to the 1970s, it was efficient consumer product manufacturing production lines that delivered cheaper products to retailer shelves. In the 1970s with the advent of the barcode, retailers replaced manufacturers as the power brokers for the industry through detailed logistical analysis of what was being sold in their stores at item level. In 2007, the power of retail was transitioned to consumer with the introduction of the iPhone from Apple. Consumers today have tremendous flexibility on their Smart devices to determine the winners and losers of the retail industry.

The same Smartphone device and our ability to travel efficiently to every corner of the world is opening more doors for each of us to discover and exploit through personal branding our own value-sharing audience. Social media has added more fuel to the niche global audience building fire, especially as we migrate utilization to mobile devices.

A personal brand, through Smart devices and the internet, helps you identify the audience that shares your passions and ideas. A parallel term often used for this concept is finding your tribe.

As I pleasantly discovered, finding 'my tribe' opened doors that I was unaware were available as business opportunities. My focus on innovation and leadership was a natural evolution of my internal desires to continuously learn something new.

Turns out my sweet spot was innovation hubs such as Silicon Valley. As I evolved my personal brand, the outreach I received from startups was inspiring. This led to engagements with an amazing number of global innovators as I tracked twice a year to San Francisco to listen to their frenzied 3 minute pitches.

The Silicon Valley experience and exposure led to multiple other boards of directors and advisory roles in next generation technologies. When I accepted a CEO role for a leading security company, those same innovation lessons inspired the successful reinvention of a retail industry technology sector.

The magic of a personal brand is that 'your tribe' is also looking for people like you. In one of my favorite books, *Think and Grow Rich* by Napoleon Hill, the author introduces the concept of a 'Master Mind Group.' We all have specialized knowledge from our experiences and education, but none of us have *every* piece of knowledge to achieve our specific goals. 'Instead, you need a Master Mind Group – a group of associates who have the knowledge, advice and expertise to help you achieve your goal. No one has enough experience, education, and ability to accumulate a fortune single-handedly. You need a Master Mind group to help you shape a plan for reaching your goal.'[17]

Create Multiple Alternative Paths to Success

Some of us are blessed with knowing exactly what we want to be when we grow up but for most of us, it takes continuous experimentation to craft a successful life. I arrived in the United States at age 11 from Italy. As a closet introvert, I was not sure exactly what possibilities America would deliver.

Early teen experiments at building leadership capabilities gave impetus to a potential future in politics. But having to contribute to family finances and funding post high school education pounded the reality of near-term thinking into my life.

Being bored with a pre-law university education and discovering marketing late in the Bachelor Degree program led to a career reset. An MBA in marketing followed, but where to put it to good use was the question.

Being an introvert, frankly I was surprised by the first professional position that I accepted out of university: selling cash registers. Yet I adapted quickly and with a strong mentor had a very successful sales career.

Industry marketing and product management roles followed and I started steadily climbing that desired corporate ladder. But as the introduction to this book pointed out, not all rungs on that ladder to success can be easily climbed.

The disappointment in not getting that major promotion led to the creation of my personal brand. I had no idea at the time where a personal brand would take me. In the early days, it was just an experiment to test whether my personal ideas on innovation and leadership could find a global audience that would create alternate paths to success.

Yet that leap of faith into the unknown, exposing personal ideas for others to comment on and even criticize, was the magic spark that I needed to test alternate futures. As it turned out, what I chose actually elevated my presence and value within the same existing employer that did not give me the coveted promotion. More importantly, it started bringing new audiences to my ideas, audiences whose potential I am still expanding on today.

Always remember, no matter your age, it is never too late to get started experimenting and intentionally creating multiple potential paths to success. In my writings, you will see that I had a Plan A, Plan B, Plan C and sometimes even a Plan D in terms of which direction I wanted to take my career. A personal brand which I should have started much earlier accelerated the right choices to a more fulfilling direction of my life. It's never too late, but it's late if you don't take that first step NOW.

Increase Trust and Credibility

In his book, *The 7 Habits of Highly Effective People*, Stephen Covey[18] wrote, 'Trust is the glue of life. It's the most essential ingredient in effective communication. It's the foundational principle that holds all relationships. When the trust account is high, communication is easy, instant, and effective.'

Among the definitions in Dictionary.com[19] for the word 'trust,' you will find: reliance on the integrity, strength, surety, etc of a person or thing; confident expectation of something; hope. Because it creates credibility, trust is the most critical element that builds successful personal brands.

In 2011, Gaford and Drapeau published a formula that defines trustworthiness. Their research had credibility plus reliability plus intimacy divided by self-orientation as the formula equalling trustworthiness. Credibility is earned by expertise and by being clear about your limitations. Reliability is the result of consistency and dependability. Intimacy is not about personal details, but rather understanding the sensitivity of others. Self-orientation is the motive or degree to which you focus on your own concerns when interacting with others.[20] With the correct orientation, credibility, reliability and intimacy are important components to increased trustworthiness.

Research conducted by The Institute of Leadership and Management found that industries with the lowest internal trust, ie the employees did not trust their own organizations, were in turn not trusted much by the public either.[21] In other words, there is a strong link between consumer and employee trust levels and consumers avoiding organizations they do not trust.

I am sharing this level of detail on trust because it is the most important element you need to consider in building a successful personal brand.

To build personal trust, Galford and Drapeau shared a 5 stage process:[22]

1. **ENGAGING** Find common ground and relate to other people
2. **LISTENING** Build trust by showing that one cares enough to invest time in listening.
3. **FRAMING** Make sure that one understands the core of what the other person is conveying, and let him or her know it.
4. **ENVISIONING** Look to the future and identify an optimistic and achievable outcome and help others to visualize the benefits of that outcome.
5. **COMMITTING** Both parties agree and commit to moving towards the envisioned future.

The elements described in these 5 stages are actually a roadmap for communicating your personal brand. Fundamentally, your brand stands or falls on the level of trust that it delivers.

Curiosity and Invaluable Continuous Learning

A major side benefit of creating a personal brand is that, properly executed, it leads to continuous exploration of new ideas and concepts to elevate its value. Curiosity and continuous learning are parallel concepts that are critical to creating your brand.

As a *Psychology Today*[23] article pointed out, 'If you suspect that curious kids fare better in careers and life, you're right – for a variety of reasons. Research suggests that intellectual curiosity has as big an effect on performance as hard work. When put together, curiosity and hard work account for success just as much as intelligence. Another study found that people who were curious about a topic retained what they learned for longer periods of time. And even more impressive, research has linked curiosity to a wide range of important adaptive behaviors, including tolerance of anxiety and uncertainty, positive emotions, humor, playfulness, out-of-box thinking and a noncritical attitude – all attributes associated with healthy social outcomes.'

In the movie *The Shawshank Redemption*,[24] there is a famous line delivered by Morgan Freeman, 'It comes down to a simple choice really. Get busy living or get busy dying.' Curiosity is the get busy living magic formula to identifying what's next.

We are privileged in this age for the many tools at our disposal that enable us to learn something new every single day. The Smartphone as the mobile gateway to the internet is the new goldmine to success. In building my personal brand, I have made it a priority to learn something novel every single day, or meet a new individual, or explore the connectivity between ideas that enter into my mind.

If I am standing in line at the airport, I scan news aggregator apps for new concepts and ideas to link to my personal brand. I constantly forward articles to myself for deeper reading or sharing with my audience, if the content is original and differentiated. It does not necessarily have to be all about you. Sharing other people's concepts and ideas upgrades the value of your personal brand.

The goldmine to success is identifying the patterns BETWEEN ideas and leveraging the emerging convergence trends to dramatically increase your personal and professional value. Continuous learning, which is the output of curiosity, means that you can constantly enhance your personal brand with content your audience will find thought provoking and value adding.

Take Control of Your Online Narrative

Social media is an important starting point in controlling the narrative for your personal brand. As you will discover later, selecting the appropriate social media channel for delivering the most impactful content is one of the most critical elements to monetizing your brand.

Because of social media, whether you like it or not, you have an online reputation. That reputation builds over time and is based on the consistency and variety of the material that you post.

When you undertake the journey in creating a personal brand, you are consciously re-evaluating your current online presence in terms of what it is today and, by design, aligning it to the value you want to create for your personal brand. This means revisiting the content already posted and potentially updating or revising it.

More importantly, it means creating a detailed strategy to control how the messaging and narrative moves forward. Also, as you will discover later, there are supplemental tools that you can add to your branding mix that elevate your importance in search engines and make your brand more valuable.

The explosion of social media means that lots of words (and pictures) have already introduced you to this world. Creating a personal brand means that you take control of the online narrative and increase its value over time.

Increase Top-of-Mind Awareness

In 2022, the average American[25] was exposed to 4,000 to 10,000 ads per day which is nearly double what it was in 2007 and over 5 times that of the 1970s.[26] The average internet user is shown 1,707 ads each month.[27] Google, Amazon and Facebook account for 64% of all USA digital ad spending.[28] The purpose of all these ads is to increase top-of-mind awareness.

In building a personal brand, of course, you would never reach these volumes, but the strategy is the same. In a world full of digital noise, you need to stand out. There are unique strategies that you can pursue that can differentiate your personal brand.

If, as I did, you begin your personal branding journey while working for a corporation, increasing your top-of-mind awareness pays dividends for the company you are working with and builds your own expertise credibility in the world at the same time. The optimal strategy is to create a personal brand that supports your current employer, but also elevates your visibility outside the company. This is indeed possible and, as in my case, leads to major senior leadership engagement where your employer values your insights and even asks you to teach them your strategies to elevate their own brand.

Top-of-mind awareness is built through consistent, focused, differentiated content delivery through the channels that you identify as optimal to your brand. Where possible, to increase the odds that the content is shared, I even tagged the employer that I was working with. In turn, at all levels, including senior leadership, they reposted or added comments to the content.

In a 2022 internet minute or just 60 seconds, 16 million texts and over 231 million emails are sent, 500 new hours of video are loaded on YouTube, nearly 6 million searches take place on Google, over 347,000 X posts are generated, and we spend $443,000 on Amazon.[29]

In 2022, the amount of data created, captured and consumed daily globally was 97 zettabytes and that number is expected to increase to 181 zettabytes by 2025. As a point of reference, a zettabyte is equivalent to 1 trillion gigabytes.[30]

The takeaway from this technology download is that the world's digital footprint will dramatically increase. The sooner you begin your branding journey to establish top-of-mind credibility, the higher the personal brand monetary value you will achieve.

Leave a Positive Lasting Legacy

The American polymath Benjamin Franklin who was a writer, scientist, inventor, statesman, printer publisher, forger and political philosopher once said, 'If you would not be forgotten as you are dead, either write something worth reading or do something worth writing.'[31]

No one is asking you to match the wide breadth of activities pursued by Benjamin Franklin, but whether you are consciously aware of it or not, your personal legacy is being defined every single day. It includes the choices you make, what you post on social media, how you interact with friends and family, and even the career you choose and the work ethic you bring to it.

In building a personal brand, you are actively choosing to more clearly define how your brand will be perceived today and the legacy it will leave behind when you are gone.

A personal brand forces you to test and learn, adapt and build, incremental value towards a much stronger durable legacy. Increased curiosity and continuous learning give you greater ideas on actions you can take to building more success, overcoming obstacles and constructing a better life that are the foundational elements of our future legacy.

Looking back to how I got started with my personal brand, initial attempts were crude, short, experimental and evolutionary in the topics explored. Yet I quickly discovered the Power of Three – which we will discuss in future chapters – ultimately evolved into an approach that has created a lasting leadership legacy.

Legacy is not a one-time event or one place. It's the accumulation of ideas that help enrich your life and inspire others to join the same journey of discovery towards fulfilling lasting experiences. As Gary Vaynerchuk said, 'Please think about your legacy because you are (already) writing it every day.'[2]

COMPANY VERSUS PERSONAL BRANDING

Advertising has trained us to be brand conscious. According to Interbrand,[3] in 2022, the top five most valuable global product brands were Apple, Microsoft, Amazon, Google and Samsung. The top five most valuable retail brands were Ikea, Zara, H&M, eBay and Sephora. For luxury, the top five were Louis Vuitton, Chanel, Hermes, Gucci and Cartier.

As you read these product branding leadership lists, think of the emotion that each of the brands reveals in your mind about their particular business model and products. For instance, innovation in companies like Apple, Amazon and Google; scarcity in needing to shop now in stores such as Zara as you might not find that special fashion tomorrow; the exclusivity of luxury brands as well as the sometimes hidden pride in actually owning their products. Successful corporate brands over time created a special cache feeling in each of us which evolved into loyalty and in turn makes each of these companies even more successful.

The value of the Top 100 Global Brands in the latest Interbrand[4] research crossed over $3 trillion. For 2022, it was the, 'Fastest rate of brand value growth ever recorded, demonstrating the growing contribution a company's brand has in driving economic success.'

Take another look at the list of brands that are now the world product leaders. You might be surprised that the average age of the top five most valuable company brands is only 39.6 years.[5] As Interbrand, points out, 'Competition is fierce and the speed at which the world's most relevant businesses can scale is unprecedented. So, too, is the risk. In the two decades since we launched Best Global Brands, only 36 companies have remained in our Top 100 Table. More than 140 have dropped off in the intervening years, including staple brands such as Nokia, AOL, Yahoo! and MTV.'[6]

Considering that Western Europe[7] leads the world with the average life expectancy of an individual person at 82.7 years, amazingly, the age in the top five brands is less than half that of the average person in Western Europe.[8] Advances in technology are shortening the life of corporate brands and this is good news for you as those same technologies can be leveraged to increase the value of your personal brand.

In other words, as with everything else, technology is speeding up the pace at which successful brands are created, monetized and elevated. The same is now possible with your personal brand and, in many cases, you can leverage the success lessons of the major product brands.

Your personality is your company brand. The value you create around it is totally in your control as long as you fine-tune the formulas we will explore in this book and craft them into your dream future. Remember, if you dream it, with hard work, you will achieve it.

SOCIAL MEDIA AND YOUR PERSONAL BRAND

More than half of the world (59%) now uses social media. Usage is even higher in Western developed markets.[9] In the United States, as of January 2023, nearly 74% of the population was on social media; in Western Europe it is even higher at nearly 84%; even Eastern Asia which includes China has a 72% social media penetration.[10]

On average, in 2022, each of us spent 147 minutes (nearly 2.5 hours) PER DAY reading and sharing on social media networks.[11] This equates to more than 37 days in a year or more than a month each year.

The odds are extremely high that if you are reading this book, you are using social media and are one of those active users. You probably never think about it, but everything that you place on social media is defining your personal brand.

So, before posting that wild picture that impacts your brand, consider this:

o 71% of US hiring decision-makers agree that looking at candidates' social media profiles is an effective way to screen applicants.[12]
o 70% believe employers should screen all applicants' social media profiles, while the majority (67%) say they use social networking sites to research potential job candidates.[13]
o For those using social networking to research candidates, more than half(55%) have found content that caused them not to hire the applicant.[14]

Social media is an important element in building a professional personal brand, but it also carries risks, especially if, historically, you did not pay attention to the content being published. Selecting the appropriate platform to elevate your value is one of the most critical steps in building presence that will increase your success. It begins by understanding the audience of each particular channel and delivering planned content that increases your market value, topics which will be discussed in more detail in later chapters.

SUMMARY

o   Branding has evolved substantially and continues to do so. We are on the threshold of the next megatrend as technology makes it possible to create powerful personal brands.

o   Personal branding is the deliberate crafting of your public persona, which includes all content created to shape it. Succinctly, the end result of a well-executed personal brand is greater autonomy. You are in control of your destiny and not your employer.

o   Company brands such as Zara, Louis Vuitton etc over time created a special cache feeling in each of us which evolved into loyalty and in turn made each of these companies even more successful. Technology today makes it possible to export the success lessons of these companies in building your personal brand.

o   Everything you place on social media defines your personal brand and can potentially have a negative impact on your career.

o   A strategically well-executed personal brand will turn your name into a valuable monetizable asset, find you a valuable value-sharing global audience, create multiple alternative paths to success, increase trust and credibility, lead to more curiosity and invaluable continuous learning, allow you to take control of your online narrative, increase top-of-mind awareness, and leave a lasting positive legacy.

o   Your global audience is out there, providing both business and personal growth opportunities.

o   Your motivation level will dramatically increase when you link to individuals that have similar passions and desires to improve from where they started.

o   Branding is a continuously iterative process that inspires you to continuously improve rather than finding any magic stopping point.

REFLECTIONS

ARE YOU COMFORTABLE WITH WHAT
PEOPLE SAY ABOUT YOU WHEN YOU
ARE NOT IN THE ROOM?

WHICH ARE YOUR FAVORITE
COMPANY BRANDS AND
WHY ARE YOU LOYAL TO THEM?

WHAT LEGACY DO YOU WANT
TO LEAVE TO THE WORLD?

DO YOU REALLY HAVE THAT
BURNING DESIRE TO CREATE A
VALUABLE PERSONAL BRAND?

CHAPTER 2

WHAT DO YOU STAND FOR?

'YOUR VISION WILL BECOME CLEAR
ONLY WHEN YOU LOOK INTO YOUR HEART.
HE WHO LOOKS OUTSIDE, DREAMS.
HE WHO LOOKS INSIDE, AWAKENS.'

CARL JUNG

Have there been times when your inner fire has been lit, you became agitated, and you took a stand on something that you truly believed in? At the core of that feeling were beliefs that have, to date, shaped your personality to date and your personal brand.

As we will explore in this chapter, one of the greatest benefits of creating a personal brand is the parallel, highly valuable journey of more clearly identifying what you truly stand for. Understanding your core principles and leveraging them in building a differentiated brand is what leads to greater life satisfaction.

Fake personal brands always fail for the fundamentals inside the individual will eventually lower the mask to reveal the true self. Your core principles and values are your most important asset for they are the foundation for lasting success that almost magically attract new opportunities through a personal brand.

The modern world has introduced confusion with most of us not clearly understanding or leveraging our core values. When we meet a stranger and we introduce ourself, most of us focus on our name, typically followed by our occupation. There is so much more that we sometimes suppress to try to impress the world. Yet what's churning inside each of us, properly channelled, optimizes careers, leads to much greater levels of happiness and creates powerful personal brands.

BEGIN WITH YOUR PRINCIPLES AND VALUES

Principles are those deep within you values which in turn are the foundation of what you stand for. Living, and more importantly showcasing, them in your day-to-day activities builds trust which is the most critical element in building a personal brand.

There is a reason they are called values. Very simply, these are what you value most and under the right conditions, spark amazing fires within you.

Those potential values that shape your principles culminate in a lengthy list. A few to consider could be:[1]

o Acceptance	o Humor	o Spirituality
o Fulfillment	o Security	o Excellence
o Power	o Community	o Orderliness
o Achievement	o Integrity	o Trust
o Fun	o Self-expression	o Family
o Privacy	o Creativity	o Partnership
o Adventure	o Leadership	o Truth
o Holistic living	o Self-realization	o Freedom
o Recognition	o Curiosity	o Personal growth
o Altruism	o Loyalty	o Walking the talk
o Honesty	o Service	o Friendship
o Respect	o Environment	o Physical
o Commitment	o Openness	appearance

This is by no means an exhaustive list. Rather, it is a starting point to help you evaluate deep insight into your own psyche, understand what drives you and enables you to identify your own valuable principles.

Having a long list of values is not necessarily optimal. Quite the opposite. If the list is too long, you have not clearly identified your true core principles and values.

I would highly recommend that you take the time to create your own personal list of core values as this is the critical first step in crafting a successful personal brand. Matching your core principles and values to your personal brand is what drives increased success.

When principles and a personal brand are aligned, magic happens. Delivery of your leadership content seems more natural. Finding content to enhance your message gets easier. Your personality will exude trust and confidence which increases the value of your brand.

Think again in terms of the Power of Three. In other words, work diligently to identify your top three core principles and values.

My top three principles are:

o INTEGRITY

o CURIOSITY

o LEADERSHIP

They rattled out of my mind and onto these pages without even thinking about them as they are the elements that have continuously evolved my personal brand.

The top three, by the way, are not static. They can change over time as you mature, discover new passions, or even decide, for example, to change careers.

Key to identifying your core principles and values is writing them down; keep them visible both on paper and in your mind constantly; at the beginning revisit them at least once a week; cross out or add based on actions or feedback received.

Reaching your personal top three core principles is the critical start. 'What you value, you become. Values guide your life – if you know what they are.'[2] Embrace that feeling of freedom in knowing that you are in control and are building on what fundamentally is within to create a future valuable personal brand.

NEVER FORGET WHERE YOU CAME FROM

What shapes our core principles and values are our experiences. No matter at what part of your life this book finds you, you are an incremental masterpiece of experiences that over time have brought you to this current state.

The human mind is amazing as it has a way of letting you continuously remember and enhance great experiences and sporadically remind you of the bad ones to keep it all in perspective. This has been the case for my own life.

I grew up in a small mountain town of nearly 1600 people in central Italy. I was a shy child but one day, in either kindergarten or first or second grade, I was asked to be in a play. The introvert that day decided to act out and be vivacious and expressive. The positive reaction from the audience was magical and this was the start of the closet introvert taking bolder steps to express his personality.

I did not know it at the time, but as immigrants my parents taught me many cultural lessons, first in Switzerland where I spent my summers as a young child while my parents worked, and at age 11 in the United States, where they opened my eyes to the big world, one that was full of possibilities for positive growth.

Life in the US was difficult at first as the culture shock was almost too much to overcome. But in my third year there, that vivacious kindergartner or early grades individual came out again when I discovered that singing naughty Italian songs at parties meant getting nice monetary tips from the audience.

A passion for retail and technology followed through university years resulting in successful careers in both. Yet I have never forgotten those early experiences that shaped my life.

The same is true for each of you. There are foundational experience elements within you that have been there from the start. As in my situation, not all of them were positive.

It is the combination of the positive and negative experiences that brought you to this moment in time. Think back and reflect on the lessons learned, the mistakes which are no longer relevant, and the joy of that feeling when you felt you were on top of the world.

Where it goes next has not yet been written. The future for all of us is a blank page. But this is the time to write your own memorable living masterpiece that will outlive you through a valuable personal brand.

WEAKNESSES DO NOT DEFINE YOU

What you firmly believe in through your core principles, enhanced by your experiences, are the formula elements that shape your strengths and weaknesses. Let's get the elephant out of the room immediately and discuss weaknesses.

Multiple research studies confirm that we tend to focus more on our weaknesses. 'People perceive their weaknesses as more malleable than their strengths. Moreover, motivation also influences how people see themselves in the future, such that they expect their present strengths to remain constant, but they expect their present weaknesses to improve in the future. Several additional findings suggest the motivational nature of these effects: the difference in perceived malleability for strengths versus weaknesses was only observed for the self, not for other people. When the desirability of possessing a certain trait was manipulated, that trait was perceived to be more malleable when it was depicted as undesirable. And these different beliefs that people have about how malleable their traits are, and how they will develop in the future, were associated with their desire for change, which is higher for weaknesses versus strengths.'[3]

Let's face it, most of us have a negativity bias that shows its head more often than we would like. Research points to evolution as the source for this bias as our ancestors, thousands of years ago, were exposed to serious threats such as large predators and being attentive to the negative meant survival.[4]

My least favorite activity during my corporate career was the annual performance review where focus always tended to be on 'those areas of improvement.' I can probably guarantee that getting that annual business inquisition is not one of your favorite activities either.

As the *Harvard Business Review* has pointed out, 'It is a paradox of human psychology that while people remember criticism, they respond to praise. The former makes them defensive and therefore unlikely to change, while the latter produces confidence and the desire to perform better.'[5]

Loathing those annual performance reviews was one of the motivators in creating my own personal brand. Along with not getting that coveted promotion, they were a reminder that the power to showcase your value is inside of each of us.

The individual on the other side of the table focusing on those 'areas of improvement' does not fully understand your true potential. Besides, you as an individual may not find your current role stimulating and are not giving it your best.

Weaknesses do not define you. Each of us has consequential strengths which, when channelled properly through a personal brand, differentiate and elevate performance to unbelievable possibilities for success and happiness.

CORE PRINCIPLES AND EXPERIENCES ARE YOUR STRENGTHS

We do need to pay attention to our weaknesses and understand them, but as research has confirmed, 'When we focus on developing our strengths, we grow faster than when trying to improve our weaknesses. Plus, people who use their strengths are happier, less stressed, and more confident.'[6]

Believing in your strengths leads to greater self-awareness and to a happier life. Data confirms that leaders who perceive themselves to be effective are more likely to demonstrate good leadership. Those who embrace their capabilities and acknowledge the input of their teams are more likely to become better leaders.[7]

'Finding and harnessing your strengths bring you closer to a more fulfilled life. A case study shows that those who discover their strengths interact with the world differently. Focusing on the things we do well allows us to get the most out of life. Studies on strengths-based development training found that harnessing your strengths improves confidence and a sense of direction in life. In addition to gaining a better understanding of their life purpose, people who focus on their best traits are more likely to believe in themselves and their abilities. Moreover, research on authentic happiness found that people who have identified the things they're good at and actively pursue experience more positive emotions, increased engagement and higher levels of well-being.'[8]

Identifying your strengths is critical to happiness and building a powerful personal brand. Leveraging your strengths focuses your mind on what you are good at and, by doing this, actually improves your performance over time. This, in turn, builds an even stronger personal brand.

IDENTIFY YOUR PERSONAL STRENGTHS

There are multiple strategies that can be leveraged to identify your personal strengths.

o Start by thinking beyond just work traits and focus on your personality.

o Read the many articles on the internet on this subject, some of which are included in the reference section of this book.

o Ask people you trust for their direct feedback.

o Pay attention when people offer praise and look for patterns across comments from different individuals.

- There are lots of personality and other testing programs online that are either free or you can buy to assess your strengths.

- If you have been employed, those personal annual reviews often have questions where you provide answers in these areas.

- You can simply make a list of what you enjoy doing and what motivates you to do more.

- Keep a journal of experiences, both negative and positive. Review the entries to identify your strengths.

The most important step to this process is gathering the data to qualify and, just like principles and values, working to narrow down to your most important value adding strengths. There should be a correlation, by the way, between your strengths and your core values for their intersection is where a powerful personal brand can be developed.

As with core values and principles, you need to spend time to identify as you narrow the focus to your most important and valuable strengths. Think again top three.

My general top three strengths which I have now crafted into a personal brand are:

- RETAIL

- INNOVATION

- LEADERSHIP

If you Google my name, my personal website will surface with these three words summarizing the content.

As is the case with my top three identified strengths, these can be general in nature. The messaging you deliver around your strengths is what narrows their focus and makes your brand stand out.

Understanding your strengths is critical to building your audience or tribe of followers. The closer your consistently delivered messaging is to your strengths:

o The more passion you will have in the research.

o The greater your audience will perceive value.

o The stronger your brand will become over time.

YOUR PERSONAL STRENGTHS BECOME USPS

A USP is a Unique Selling Proposition and it is the foundation for monetizing your personal brand. All of us have strengths, but it is USPs that will show you the money.

A USP is what differentiates you from the competition. 'It's a specific and clear benefit that makes your business stand out when compared to other businesses in your market. Forming an opinionated and deliberate USP helps focus your marketing strategy and influences messaging, branding, copywriting, and other marketing decisions, and influences prospective customers.'[9]

When you hear company names such as Nike, Coca-Cola, Zara, Starbucks, McKinsey, Gartner and many others, conceptually the value and loyalty for their products comes into your mind. Each of these companies has unique features in their business models that differentiate them from the competition and made them highly successful.

The same is true for personal brands. You must stand for unique value and differentiation from others in the market to grow and monetize your audience. There are hybrid personal brands that blend personality and actual products and these can often be seen in celebrities that leverage their name and sell incremental products into the market.

My focus with you on this personal branding journey is to help you figure out what you stand for, beginning with your principles and values. Subsequently, we will identify your personal strengths and turn them into unique selling propositions (USPs) that elevate your current career and set you up for alternate future options so you can live the life of your dreams.

Now, let's analyze what we mean by Unique Selling Propositions:

o **UNIQUE** Success requires differentiated services or content and be perceived as highly valuable to your audience.

o **SELLING** The old adage that 'we are all in sales' is true. Your message to the market needs to be clear and you need to sell it through your personal brand.

o **PROPOSITION** Vocabulary.com defines a proposition as a proposed plan of action or a detailed suggestion.[10]

Each of these words – Unique, Selling, Proposition – are critical to executing a successful personal brand. You must identify uniqueness leveraging your passions and strengths; you must market those ideas which today is a lot easier starting with social media; and most importantly, you must implement a plan of action that consistently showcases your differentiated compelling value.

For my personal brand, the general categories are retail, innovation, and leadership, but over time I have fine-tuned the messaging into projecting being a visionary of where the retail industry evolves next, emerging technologies that are driving transformation, and the leadership required for success.

When Silicon Valley became a primary audience, their interest allowed me to retire 10 years earlier than planned in order to explore advancement of innovation. Subsequently, both industry groups and larger companies have welcomed my consulting assistance on strategy, new products, customer ideation, public relations and marketing.

PERSONAL BRANDING AND YOUR EXISTING CAREER

Personal branding is a door opener to optional possibilities of how you want to grow as an individual. In creating a personal brand, it is not a requirement that you must leave your existing career to become an independent entrepreneur.

If you are one of those individuals that greatly enjoys climbing the corporate ladder, I would strongly urge you to increase the odds that you will go higher by creating a personal brand that enhances your existing career.

This was the case when I started my own personal brand. As I showcased retail innovation leadership to the market through content on my social media channels, corporate leadership noticed and actually supported my initiatives.

Greater visibility led to greater research on the future of the retail industry which I then transitioned into my *Disruptive Future of Retail* keynote presentation that I still regularly update.

As my online audience grew, invitations followed to senior leadership meetings to explain what I was doing and unveil my formula. Senior leaders started duplicating my approach to elevate their own personal brand. They also regularly showed up in my content, supporting and reposting it.

Especially in a large corporation, it is easy to get lost and feel like you are just another cog in the wheel of uncertainties. As *Harvard Business Review* reminds us, a personal brand gives you impetus to 'being up-to-date in your industry, making you more resilient and adaptable. It means being recognized for your unique self and skills, and increasing your visibility, access to opportunities, and growth. A positive personal brand is beneficial to both you and your organization.'[11]

Once you create a personal brand within a corporation, take the initiative to showcase it within the company. Volunteer for projects that leverage your now increased personal value. Publicly support company initiatives that elevate the value of your own brand. Focus especially on projects that are customer or revenue generating facing as they will carry even more weight in upward visibility.

What you stand for at work is just as important as an independent career as an entrepreneur. The greatest defense against worries in being part of a 'reduction in force' is an offense by increasing your value to the corporation. The plus of executing a personal brand is that it both makes you more valuable in your existing position, but more importantly, opens your eyes to multiple potential future opportunities for personal and professional growth.

ARE YOU LOST? DON'T WORRY, YOU'RE NOT ALONE

You may be at a point or time in your career where either in the corporate world or personally you feel lost and unmotivated. You are not alone.

Traditional norms in helping us define value have changed dramatically in recent years. Gone are the days of going to work for one employer and making that a lifetime experience. In the United States, consider the following:[12]

o The median employee tenure is now 4.3 years for men and 4 years for women.

o 91% of millennials expect to change jobs every 3 years.

o Nearly 75% of the Gen X generation expect to return to school.

o Only 14% of people feel they landed a dream job.

o 70% of the workforce is actively looking for a change in career.

The world of work has indeed changed and become riskier. The pandemic accelerated negative trends and added additional stress. Many of us are constantly reassessing what motivates us to keep moving forward.

Motivation has a major impact on defining what we stand for today and where we want to put our emphasis for growth tomorrow. The fire needs to burn in each of us to improve and much of the fuel in the past was the perceived rewards for hard work.

In his book, *Drive*, Daniel Pink charts a new path for motivation in the workplace. We are no longer living in primitive survival or in a culture of reward and punishment. Traditional 'carrot and stick' approaches no longer work in a globally connected fast moving innovative world.[13]

According to Pink, the new motivational model requires:[14]

o **AUTONOMY** The ability to direct your own life and work when, how and with whom. Autonomy motivates us creatively without limited corporate conformity.

o **MASTERY** This is the desire to continuously improve along with the feeling of unlimited potential rewards for the hard work to get there.

o **PURPOSE** This is the understanding of the 'big picture' and believing in its positive possibilities. The mission of the corporation, in other words, aligns with the individual.

If you are feeling lost in a corporation or in your own life, the above trio of motivational elements are a critical start to improvement. Autonomy, mastery and purpose are elements that more clearly define what you stand for within a corporation. More importantly, these elements will help you find yourself in your drive to create a powerful personal brand, first inside a corporation and, as I did, pursue alternate paths to a lasting legacy.

Briefly mentioned earlier was the idea of asking others for direct feedback about you as an individual. This valuable step requires further explanation as it will influence both your current career and where you take your personal brand in the future.

My first professional position post two university degrees was in selling cash registers for NCR Corporation. Following intensive in-class training sessions on the basics of selling technology, I was assigned both a territory and a sales mentor. The sales veteran that was my senior opened initial doors for me, watched me present solutions to retailers, provided coaching, and positively criticized mistakes to drive improvement. This special individual is still a friend today and although we live far apart, I often think of the life lessons learned from our joint sales calls.

Being a closet introvert, sales in a business-to-business (B2B) was not something I was comfortable with. The encouragement from my sales senior was invaluable. In our working relationships, he also urged me to experiment with new approaches. For instance, I was the first in the region to create a success newsletter that I would share with my customers on how they were positively leveraging NCR technology.

Leveraging the experience of my mentor and innovating the sales process by highlighting the successes of my customers led to a successful short sales career. I exceeded quota in three out of the three sales years and was recognized through the prestigious career lifting NCR Century Club sales rewards program. Promotions followed in both industry marketing and product management.

As you progress in your career, strive to create a core set of advisors to provide counsel along the way to help fine-tune what you stand for. Leverage social media to follow your desired influencers and industry experts. Ask to interview some of these experts and influencers as a learning experience for your career.

Reach out regularly to individuals you trust. Test major new ideas or concepts with them first. Ask them for references and introductions to others that may have greater knowledge on your ideas.

Around the world, I am fortunate to have an extensive network of individuals always open to offer their insights. It is never too early or too late to engage an inner circle to help you frame out how to increase the value of your personal brand.

DETERMINE THE PERSONAL BRAND YOU WANT TO CREATE

My favorite lines in English literature are from *A Tale of Two Cities* by Charles Dickens:[15]

> *'It was the best of times, it was the worst of times, it was the age of wisdom, it was the age of foolishness, it was the epoch of belief, it was the epoch of incredulity, it was the season of Light, it was the season of Darkness, it was the spring of hope, it was the winter of despair, we had everything before us, we had nothing before us...'*

Today is the best of times, it is the age of wisdom now being enhanced by Artificial Intelligence (AI), it is the epoch of belief in endless possibilities of ideas through a highly connected world, it is the spring of hope as in each of us greater individuality is possible; we do have everything before us, we just need to figure out what exactly we want to be when we grow up.

There is no shortage of ideas today as what business to actually start or to what level we want to take our corporate career. As an example, in the United States alone, 4.4 million new businesses are started every year. For 2022, that new enterprises figure was over 5 million.[16]

Determining the brand you want and turning it into either a strategy that enhances your current career or creating multiple other exits to new ventures paths, begins with:

1. Figuring out who you are by spending time understanding your core principles and values.

2. Leveraging your experiences to find areas that you perceive need improvement.

3. Identifying clearly your strengths and focus on making them stronger.

4. Cleary defining your Unique Selling Propositions and what value difference they can generate.

5. Experimenting with personal branding within your current company and leveraging the lessons learned to fine-tune who you stand for.

6. Finding your own autonomy, mastery, and purpose to motivate you to the next level.

7. Actively seeking mentors and advisors to provide feedback on your journey to date and test new ideas.

8. Crystalizing from the above the top three which your personal brand will stand for.

9. Defining your audience, as we will discuss further in later chapters.

10. Embracing networking to find your global audience or tribe which will also be discussed further in later chapters.

Taking these steps looks simple, but it requires focus and dedication in execution. In the beginning, it will feel challenging, but as you dig deeper, I promise you, it will get easier, especially as you leverage the detailed success formula in this book.

A personal brand is a public expression of your passions. Re-read this chapter a few times and write out a response to each of the 10 steps. It's an amazing journey when the fire inside of you burns hot and you channel who you truly are to the world.

A LIFE WITH NO REGRETS

A favorite personal quote that I have used continuously in both articles and public speaking is, 'It's not where you started that matters, it's where you finish that makes all the difference.'

In her book, *The Top Five Regrets of the Dying*, Bronnie Ware, quoting from her summary blog, lists:[17]

1. *I wish I'd had the courage to live a life true to myself, not the life others expected of me.* 'Most people had not honored even a half of their dreams and had to die knowing that it was due to choices they had made, or not made.'

2. *I wish I hadn't worked so hard.* 'By simplifying your lifestyle and making conscious choices along the way, it is possible to not need the income that you think you do. And by creating more space in your life, you become happier and more open to new opportunities, ones more suited to your new lifestyle.'

3. *I wish I'd had the courage to express my feelings.* 'We cannot control the reactions of others. However, although people may initially react when you change the way you are by speaking honestly, in the end it raises the relationship to a whole new and healthier level. Either that or it releases the unhealthy relationship from your life. Either way, you win.'

4. *I wish I had stayed in touch with my friends.* 'It is common for anyone in a busy lifestyle to let friendships slip. But when you are faced with your approaching death, the physical details

of life fall away. People do want to get their financial affairs in order if possible. But it is not money or status that holds the true importance for them. They want to get things in order more for the benefit of those they love.'

5. **I wish that I had let myself be happier.** 'Fear of change had them pretending to others, and to their selves, that they were content. When deep within, they longed to laugh properly and have silliness in their life again.'

More succinctly, let's reflect back to Stephen Covey's book, *The 7 Habits of Highly Effective People* and more specifically Habit 2: 'Begin with the End in Mind.' This he names as the habit of personal leadership with a clear understanding of your desired direction and destination. By keeping the end in mind, you focus on the most important.[18]

In explaining Habit 2, Covey asks the reader to imagine you are attending your own funeral three years from now. Four people will provide a eulogy including a family member, a close friend, a work associate and a spiritual or community leader. As an exercise, Covey asks that each of us makes a list of what we would like each person to say at the funeral. Finally, he recommends that the characteristics, virtues and skills we want to hear in the eulogy form part of our personal mission statement.[19]

This last section may seem morbid, but I include it for the following reasons.

1. I share multiple regrets of dying today because I started my personal branding journey too late in life.

2. I worry about my eulogy as I allowed work for others to dictate my personal value for too long. Family, yes, was always important, but I sacrificed much including missing important milestones to chase up that golden corporate ladder.

Do NOT make the same mistakes.

Personal branding will help you re-assess what is important and the sooner you take this step, the better it will be for your future. The process of defining yourself is not a cakewalk. It will question everything that you have done to date. It will lead to temporary false paths.

The discovery of who you really are, however, will be transformational. I remind myself every single day that I am just getting started and because of my personal brand, I NOW know what I stand for. I do dream, but I look inside more and test new ideas constantly in fine-tuning the improved legacy that I will leave this world.

As Bronnie Ware summarized in her blog of her book *The Top Five Regrets of the Dying*, 'Life is a choice. It is YOUR life. Choose consciously, choose wisely, choose honestly. Choose happiness.'[20]

Unleash your personal brand and live a life with no regrets.

SUMMARY

o Your core principles are those deep within you values which in turn are the foundation of what you stand for. Living and, more importantly, showcasing them in your day-to-day activities builds trust which is the most critical element in building a personal brand. What you value, you become.

o What shapes our core principles and values are our experiences. No matter at what part of your life this book finds you, you are an incremental masterpiece of experiences that over time have brought you to this current state.

o Weaknesses do not define you. Each of us has consequential strengths which, when channeled properly through a personal brand, differentiate and elevate performance to unbelievable possibilities for success and happiness.

o Research confirms that when we focus on developing our strengths, we grow faster than when trying to improve our weaknesses. Plus, people who use their strengths are happier, less stressed and more confident.

o All of us have strengths, but it is Unique Selling Propositions (USPs) that will show you the money.

o The greatest defense against worries in being part of a 'reduction in force' in a company is offense by increasing your value to the corporation through a personal brand.

o Motivation has a major impact on defining what we stand for today and where we want to put our emphasis for growth tomorrow. The fire needs to burn in each of us to improve and much of the fuel in the past was the perceived rewards for hard work.

o Reach out regularly to individuals you trust. Test major new ideas or concepts with them first. Ask them for references and introductions to others that may have greater knowledge on your ideas.

o A personal brand is a public expression of your passions; 10 steps are critical to determining the brand you want to create.

o Life is a choice. It is YOUR life. It is YOUR choice. Choose consciously, choose wisely, choose honestly. Choose happiness. Unleash your personal brand and live a life with no regrets.

REFLECTIONS

WHAT ARE YOUR TOP THREE CORE
PRINCIPLES AND VALUES?

WHAT ARE YOUR TOP THREE STRENGTHS?

WHAT ARE YOUR UNIQUE QUALITIES THAT
YOU CAN POTENTIALLY TURN INTO UNIQUE
SELLING PROPOSITIONS (USPS) FOR YOUR
PERSONAL BRAND?

FROM A MOTIVATION POINT OF VIEW,
WHERE DO YOU STAND ON AUTONOMY,
MASTERY AND PURPOSE?

WHICH THREE PEOPLE THAT YOU TRUST
CAN YOU CALL TODAY FOR LIFE AND
CAREER ADVICE?

AT YOUR EULOGY, WHAT WOULD YOU
LIKE A FAMILY MEMBER, A CLOSE FRIEND,
A WORKASSOCIATE AND SPIRITUAL OR
COMMUNITY LEADER TO SAY ABOUT YOU?

CHAPTER 3

IDENTIFY YOUR IDEAL BRANDING CHANNEL

'IT IS ESTIMATED THAT A WEEK'S WORTH OF THE NEW YORK TIMES CONTAINS MORE INFORMATION THAN A PERSON WAS LIKELY TO COME ACROSS IN A LIFETIME IN THE 18TH CENTURY.'[1]

This reminder of how the world has changed comes from a favorite video – *Did You Know?* – that I have consistently shared in the past during many global presentations. It highlights the fact that today's news travels at the speed of light, with social media being a primary source. In fact, a February 2022 survey found that Gen Z individuals (the generation following millennials, born between the late 1990s and early 2010s) get much of their news from social media, with 50% reporting this is the case on daily basis.[2]

There is a reason social media is so named. 'Humans are social creatures. We live in families, we work in teams, we envision duty and purpose through religious fellowship, we negotiate through economic alliances and political coalitions, and our norms are shaped by our culture, itself an emergent property of group-living.'[3]

LINKING SOCIAL WITH MEDIA

According to a 2023 research study,[4] the top three reasons people use social media are:

1. Keeping in touch with family and friends – 47.1%
2. Filling spare time – 36.2%
3. Reading news stories – 34.2%

Linking social with media was a genius idea and let's face it, most of us are hooked on one or more channels as a result. What you must realize is that whatever you share on social media is a manifestation of what you stand for.

The internet exposes everything you publish on social media to the entire world. Most social media channels have automated or on-demand language translation of your online content. This means potentially billions of people are consciously or unconsciously experiencing an unstructured view of your personal brand. What does this mean for you? Let me tell you. It is time to take control of the narrative by understanding each of the main social media channels to optimize your personal value to the world.

We will now explore the growth of social media, the expanding list of optional channels and my favorite channels, including their pros and cons, while providing insights on selecting channels that showcase your personality.

THE WORLD OF SOCIAL MEDIA

November 15 2022 was, according to the United Nations, Day 1 of crossing over to 8 billion people living on earth.[5] It is amazing to consider how the world is now so interconnected.

In early 2023:[6]

o 5.44 billion people or 68% of the global population use mobile phones.

o 5.16 billion individuals or just over 64% of the global population are on the internet.

o 4.76 billion people or just over 60% of the global population use social media. At the date of this research, social media grew 3% from the previous year, adding another 137 million people.

The top 5 social media platforms in the world ranked by active users are:[7]

1. **FACEBOOK** 2,959 million

2. **YOUTUBE** 2,514 million

3. **WHATSAPP** 2,000 million

4. **INSTAGRAM** 2,000 million

5. **WECHAT** 1,309 million

Importantly, 3 out of the top 5 – Facebook, WhatsApp, and Instagram – are owned by Meta.

On a global basis, working age individuals now spend an average 2.5 hours per day using social media platforms. Reading or posting on our favorite platforms takes up 38% of the world's total daily online time. To put that in perspective, that working age individual on the internet now spends 30% more time using social media than watching 'traditional' television.[8]

Interesting that the top 5 countries with the highest social media online time are India, Indonesia, Mexico, Saudi Arabia, and Chile and not the United States or China where many of these platforms emerged. Not surprisingly, the older a country's population, the smaller the social media's relative share of total internet time.[9]

Overall, women tend to spend more of their online time on social media platforms. Not surprising again, the youngest devote most of their online time on social media. For those aged 16-24, nearly 43% of females and 39% of males spend their online time on the internet using social media. By comparison, for those aged 55-64, both females and males, their internet time is equal, with social media at just over 31%.[10]

On average, the world's social media users make active use of more than 7 platforms each month. As of January 2023, the top 5 social media platforms taking the most time in usage per month were:[11]

1. **TIKTOK** 23 hours and 28 minutes, up 3 hours and 51 minutes from the previous year.
2. **YOUTUBE** 23 hour and 9 minutes, down 32 minutes.
3. **FACEBOOK** 19 hours and 43 minutes, up 8 minutes.
4. **WHATSAPP** 17 hours and 20 minutes, down 1 hour and 15 minutes.
5. **INSTAGRAM** 12 hours, up 46 minutes.

If you want to sell anything in the future, social media is where you need to be given that 80% of social media marketers say consumers buy products directly from social media apps more often than brand websites or through third-party sellers. One in 5+ Gen Z, Millennial and Gen X social media users bought a product directly in a social media app in the past 3 months.[12]

If you want to be found online, you need to be on social media; 87% of social media marketers believe consumers will search for brands on social media more often than through search engines in 2023. 'The data shows that we're already on track – almost a quarter (24%) of consumers aged 18-54 already go to social media first to search for brands. This shoots up to 36% among Gen Z.'[13]

You do not need to be a celebrity to stand out on social media. Quite the opposite, brands are looking for smaller micro influencers. Eight in 10 influencer marketers currently report working with smaller creators, versus only 1 in 10 who report working with mega influencers or celebrities with over 1m followers.[14]

I believe the idea that social media is dying is a myth. Usage continues to grow each year, although at a slower pace. Additionally, as we will discover in the next section, while, starting in 2022, some legacy platforms struggled, new social media platforms are emerging regularly.

THE MANY SOCIAL MEDIA MENU CHOICES

There is no better time than the present to differentiate yourself and elevate the value of your personal and professional brand. The advent of social media along with global connectivity through the internet means there is an audience out there waiting to leverage your Unique Selling Propositions for mutual improvement.

However, time is not actually your friend, even with social media. The longer you wait, the more challenging it will become for you to find that valuable audience to monetize. As with any new technologies, once success arrives, imitators with a slightly different take on the same innovation emerge. This is already the case with social media as 100+ choices are already available.[15]

Before focusing on my favorite online channels, here are the 20 most popular social media channels for 2023.[16]

1. **FACEBOOK** 2.96 billion Monthly Active Users (MAUs). Facebook is the largest social media platform with 37% of the global population as active users. More than 200 million, primarily small businesses, use Facebook tools and 7+ million advertizers promote their business on this platform.

2. **YOUTUBE** 2.2 billion MAUs. YouTube is a video sharing platform where users watch over a billion hours of content per day.

3. **WHATSAPP** 2 billion MAUs. WhatsApp is a messaging app used in 180+ countries.

4. **INSTAGRAM** 2 billion MAUs – Instagram is a visual platform for showcasing photos and video.

5. **WECHAT** 1.26 billion MAUs Owned by Tencent, one of China's largest technology companies. This platform started as a messaging app but has evolved into an all-in-one app to message, call, shopping, pay bills, transfer money, make reservations, book taxis, and more. WeChat is the most popular social media platform in China and other parts of Asia.

6. **TIKTOK** 1 billion MAUs. Known at Douyin in China, TikTok is a short, 15 to 60 seconds video sharing app. Despite launching in only 2017, it exploded in growth and in 2021 overtook Google as the most visited internet site. Younger generations flock to TikTok with 47.4% of users in USA aged 10 to 29.

7. **WEIBO** 573 million MAUs. Weibo means 'micro blog' in Chinese. Launched by Chinese technology company Sina Corporation in 2009, it is a micro blogging platform that compares to X (formerly Twitter) and Instagram. Weibo serves a younger demographic than WeChat.

8. **KUAISHOU** 573 million MAUs. A rival to Douyin or TikTok, Kuaishou allows users to overlay text and stickers to images or videos and add sound bites. Platform is especially popular in rural parts of China.

9. **SNAPCHAT** 557 million MAUs. Snapchat focuses on photos and short videos known as snaps shared between friends with 69% of teenagers saying they use Snapchat.

10. **QZONE** 553.5 million MAUs. Another China-based app from Tencent that mixes social media networking and blogging. Users can upload multimedia, keep diaries, write blogs, play games, and stream music.

11. **TELEGRAM** 550 million MAUs. Free messaging app across multiple devices with end-to-end encryption for all activities including chats, groups, and media shared. Focus on privacy and security.

12. **QQ** 539 million MAUs. Again, owned by Tencent in China, originally it was the number one messaging app. Today, this platform allows you to decorate avatars, watch movies, play online games, stream music, shop, blog, and make payments.

13. **PINTEREST** 444 million MAUs. On Pinterest, users 'pin' photos they like to websites, product pages, blog posts, and other content on the internet. Pinterest users are 7x more likely to purchase products they have pinned.

14. **REDDIT** 430 million MAUs. Reddit has been called the front page of the internet with a mix of current events, celebrity 'ask me anything' events, and in-depth discussion on niche topics. Lots of dedicated forums on many topics.

15. **LINKEDIN** 424 million MAUs. Currently owned by Microsoft, LinkedIn has evolved from a simple job search and resumé posting engine into a professional networking platform where industry experts share content, network, and build personal brands. It's also a place where businesses can establish industry thought leadership capability.

16. **QUORA** 300 million MAUs. Quora is a community-based questions-and-answers website and app where people can discover information on a variety of topics. Questions and answers are user-ranked based on views, votes, reviews, and shares.

17. **X (FORMERLY TWITTER)** 238 million MAUs. X is a platform that strongly emphasizes real time information written in just 280 characters (140 characters in Japanese, Korean, and Chinese). Focus is on news, entertainment, sports and much more.

18. **DISCORD** 150 million MAUs. Discord is a communication platform primarily designed for gamers. It allows users to create servers, join communities, voice chat and text chat with others in real time.

19. **TWITCH** 140 million MAUs. Twitch is a live-streaming platform for gamers. Users can create a channel, stream their gameplay and interact with their audience through chat.

20. **TUMBLR** 135 million MAUs. Tumblr is a micro blogging social media site where users can share content in various formats such as text, video, GIFs, audio clips, links and more.

Several important thought-provoking patterns emerge when you analyze these top 20 global social media platforms. Among them:

o US based platforms, typically from Silicon Valley, have substantial global reach and you must consider them as potential candidates in crafting your brand.

o In recent years, China has been an epicenter of social media evolution with TikTok being the latest example taking the world by storm. Note also the expansion of these Chinese platforms into generalized immersive application that cross over into everyday activities such as shopping and paying bills. US platforms have some catching up to do in this space. If your target market for your brand is China, you have substantial choices to evaluate as optional platforms.

o As social media is evolving, specialization will continue to increase. Note the focus on specific areas such as gaming. These do provide valuable platforms, but they are niche and the rules to literally play tend to be stricter.

o Even at number 20, the audience is more than 100 million users that are active on each of these platforms EVERY single month. In other words, a large audience is available for you to market your key unique ideas and turn them into a monetized brand over time.

o Note the variety of baseline concepts for each of these platforms that if you think about it cater to our inner fire to share our thoughts and ideas in various formats. If, like me, your personality is driven by continuous learning which includes lots of research and writing, from this list you can quickly narrow down your primary and secondary platforms that allow you to create your own valuable audience. Same idea, if you are visual and prefer photos, videos, etc, there is a core set of platforms available to begin your leadership definition journey.

As we will discuss next, you should select a primary platform on which to showcase and build a personal brand. However, it is an equally appropriate strategy to leverage multiple other social media sites to supplement and increase the reach of your leadership messaging.

You can probably guess that even with selecting platforms, I follow the Power of Three. I tend to think of this as my Personal Brand Olympics:

o **GOLD** Your primary platform which drives your business model.

o **SILVER** Your supporting platform that broadens your audience and supports your primary platform.

o **BRONZE** There because it is simple to include and you want to maximize reach.

Success evolves out of experimentation. You can and should use additional social media channels to test new ideas or thought leadership concepts. Think of it as a science experiment where you have a hypothesis and undergo multiple tests to prove its validity. Like the Silicon Valley successful business model, fast failure, learning from the experience and taking the lessons learned to improvement are your ultimate goals to maintaining and improving your personal brand.

PRIMARY CHANNEL – LINKEDIN

To be successful with your personal brand, you must identify your number one channel that best fits your strengths and can be leveraged to grow an audience. This primary channel can be changed if technology evolves and / or you personally decide to change your approach to showcasing your talents. Where you start does not necessarily define where you will finish.

My primary channel when I started my personal brand was blogging, initially just on Google. It was the perfect start to fine-tune my writing skills and evolve my messaging around retail, innovation and leadership which became my top three focus areas.

You can say that LinkedIn changed my life. I discovered it first for its original use as a resumé posting site to expose my professional background, but then I noticed that the platform was evolving into a networking solution.

I do not remember exactly how it started, but I was lucky to be part of that transition. Early in their evolution, I was in contact with LinkedIn who recognized my thought leadership skills and we agreed to mutually help each other by putting my focus on their platform for publishing articles. That partnership continues today as I test advanced versions of LinkedIn through a Test Flight app.

For my personal brand, LinkedIn remains the natural primary channel. Both my career, followed by my intensive focus on innovation and leadership, are a match to the LinkedIn audience which showcases professional growth opportunities.

However, there are several limitations to Linkedin:[17]

o The largest LinkedIn user base is concentrated in the United States with 160 million people.

o The platform is used less regularly than many others. Only 9% of US users visit LinkedIn more than once a day, 12% visit every day, and 23% visit several times a week.

o The platform is free to join, but it can get expensive when fully leveraging its value.

o Some articles have expressed concerns about too much SPAM messaging.

In my case, the pros far outweigh the cons in selecting LinkedIn as my primary platform. From a number's point of view:

o Even though the user base is concentrated in the United States, the key decision makers globally that I want to reach are on the platform and it has led to a valuable network. I am close to reaching nearly 10,000 direct contacts and have 160,000+ followers on LinkedIn.

- The up and coming decision makers are on the platforms. The largest age demographics for LinkedIn are 25-30 and 30-49 years old.[18]
- It is where the money is located. The LinkedIn platform favors high income with 49% making more than $75,000 a year and 26% making $30,000 to $74,000 per year using it.[19]

Additionally, if you are a small business or are creating a personal brand, a LinkedIn profile can improve SEO ranks, as it comes across as legitimate. [17] Because you are among so many professionals, it is the best place to build credibility with both customers as well as current and past employees through testimonials and online engagements.

If your personal brand is around business, LinkedIn is the place to focus your efforts. The biggest mistake I have made is not keeping my profile updated. Make sure you revisit your profile every six months and refresh key sections including your tag line and 'about' sections plus any business changes and improvements.

SECONDARY CHANNEL – X (FORMERLY TWITTER)

I must admit that I have mixed feelings about X as a personal branding platform. It is, however, relevant as it is an instant location to post thought leadership content.

I really like the concept of limiting inputs to 280 characters as it forces you to succinctly focus on the most important component of your messaging, ie encourages critical thinking. It is also a mostly free platform and conversations are more casual.

Unlike LinkedIn which tends to focus on professionals and their career, X has evolved into a public square where everyone has an opinion. In a substantial number of cases, X has become a platform where people go to complain.

X also seems to be much more time sensitive. To be effective, you need to time your messaging to your audience. I will explain my timing formula in later chapters.

The audience is smaller with only 22% of US adults using X. Also, 44% of users are aged 18-24 and additional 31% are between 25-30 years old. Audience concentration is also higher in USA with nearly 80% being based there.[20]

For me personally, X is just an extension to the LinkedIn conversation. It is especially useful for breaking news information or timely new original content such as a blog. I spend limited time building an audience on this platform.

SECONDARY CHANNEL – FACEBOOK

As indicated earlier, at nearly 3 billion people around the world, Facebook has the largest number of active monthly users. Some additional baseline data on Facebook:[21]

o 74% of users visit Facebook at least once a day, with 51% of them visiting several times a day.

o 56.5% of Facebook users are men and 43.5% are women.

o 76% of users between the age of 18-24 and 84% between 25-30 use Facebook. 79% of people 30-49 also use it and another 68% between the ages of 50-64.

It is obvious from this data and the large global audience that Facebook is an important platform to leverage. It comes down to what you particularly want your brand to stand for and whether this is the platform on which to build it.

The platform does have excellent targeting capabilities and its ads delivery are some of the best in the world. Facebook also provides detailed analytics on your audience to help refine messaging.

Challenges at Facebook include a low conversion rate on advertising, hovering at only 1%.[22] Additionally, around the world, younger generations are leaving Facebook for other social media platforms.[23]

- In India, only 8.7% of users are in the age bracket of 13-17 and another study found that the platform is least popular among women aged 16-24.
- In the United States only 32% of teens aged 13-17 use Facebook and that number has dropped dramatically from 2014-15 when it was 71%.

Gen Z, teens, and millennials have shifted to Instagram and Snapchat as their preferred platforms.

Because of its size, Facebook is still an important social media platform. Its targeted use will depend on the brand you are trying to build and the audience you are trying to reach.

For my personal brand, Facebook is secondary to LinkedIn though I share content as it has further global reach than my primary platform. I keep my profile updated on Facebook and visit it periodically to assess engagement.

OPPORTUNISTIC CHANNEL – YOUTUBE

A trend I have been studying and a strategy I have been fine-tuning for some time is evolving my content to becoming more visual. If you need convincing, let me remind you that in 2023, around the world we watched 3.67 million YouTube videos and 167 TikTok videos in a single internet minute or, to be clearer, just 60 seconds.[24]

In the United States, YouTube ranks higher than Facebook in usage by all adults with 73% of adults using YouTube and 38% of those users reporting logging several times a day.[25]

The largest demographic for YouTube is 18-29 year olds with 91% using it. Those aged 30-49 and 13-17 also are heavy users at 87% and 85% respectively.[26]

As Google owns YouTube, posting on this platform will help your Search Engine Optimization (SEO) rankings. It has been said that a one minute video is worth 1.8 million words.[27]

- People are 27 times more likely to click on an online video ad than a static banner ad.

- X posts with videos are 6 times more likely to be shared than those with just images, and images are 150% times more like to be shared that text-only posts.

- Video content can increase intent to purchase by 82% with 73% of consumers more likely to buy after watching a branded video about a product or service.

I am beyond sold that video needs to be a component in building a professional monetizable brand. In fact, I have already invested in an in-home studio where I am producing content, but again you can simply start with your Smartphone.

My personal YouTube channel is just getting started, but I am enjoying transitioning key content to a visual format. Smartphone cameras are powerful devices that can generate great content almost instantly and increase over time the value of your personal and professional brand.

Key to a video strategy where I need additional work is advertising the content generated which can be time consuming. In my particular case, I have integrated my YouTube videos into the weekly publishing formula which will be explained in later chapters.

You also need to factor, as your video presence increases, the amount of time required to edit and professionalize your visual content. Fortunately, software which is easy to use is readily available for these tasks. In my particular case I use Wonder Share Filmora, but you can find others on the internet.

With YouTube I am just getting started and I am exploring multiple strategies including moving to shorter, more visual, content which has already proved to grow audience faster. Your brand will benefit from those candid camera moments, if you keep them professional and educational.

OPPORTUNISTIC CHANNEL – INSTAGRAM

Continuing the theme of making content more visual, you should not be surprised that I have introduced Instagram into my brand building strategy. However, it is still an opportunistic channel as I am exploring various strategies to improve the information that the audience finds valuable.

Meta owns both Facebook and Instagram. The key difference between the two platforms is the content shared. Instagram allows posting of only photos and videos. Facebook accepts videos with longer content, photos, as well as other types of media such as articles, website links and even quizzes.

Some interesting statistics about Instagram:[28]

o 63% of Instagram users login at least once a day.

o Younger people favor the platform with 72% and 67% of 13-17 and 18-29, respectively using it. This drops to 47% for 30-49 and 23% for 50–64-year olds.

o 35% of US teenagers rank Instagram as their favorite social media platform, behind only to Snapchat.

o Instagram's engagement rate is 70% higher than Facebook.

o The follower's growth rate on Instagram is 9% compared to X (formerly Twitter) 0.11%.

If you are into showcasing your photographic skills, Instagram is the platform for you. Since it relies on visual content, you will be limited on what you can share. The ideal length of captions is between 138 and 150 words. For advertising it should be less than 125 words.[29]

Another major disadvantage of Instagram is that it does not support clickable links. This makes it difficult for your audience to be directed to additional content you are trying to share beyond the actual post.

I discovered Instagram during the COVID-19 pandemic. As I was not able to travel, I decided to start sharing photos from cities around the world where I travelled and at the same time learn something new about that experience. I titled the series *It's a Small World* and periodically I publish a picture from a city or an experience and I share history or fun facts about that location or experience. The content generated for Instagram also appears on my personal website as an additional brand building activity. My particular formula for sharing on Instagram is not yet perfect and, after researching this book, I will be making further changes to the strategy to improve the effectiveness of leveraging this important visual platform.

SELECT YOUR SOCIAL MEDIA CHANNEL

When I started my journey only a few limited tools were available. Today, it is easier than ever to establish a powerful personal and professional brand.

The critical first step is having the fire within you to create a future that is fully under your control. The follow up action is to select the appropriate channels to introduce the world to your new and value improved personality.

If you recall, simplistic Google blogs were my initial attempt at brand value creation. Since then, my journey has migrated into multiple generations of a personal website and fine-tuning the utilization of social media. The research going into this book will, I know, elevate my professional brand even more.

Social media is today's magic key to telling your story on your own terms. It begins by cleaning up any mistakes of the past and removing content which does not reflect the brand you want the world to value. It is true that nothing can be erased from the internet, but removing content before aggressively introducing your new brand is a good first step.

As this chapter has illustrated, the number of social channels available to tell your personal and professional story is growing. That is good and bad news.

The good news is that as channels are splintering or new ones are emerging, they are fine-tuning the audience that attracts them. This means, if you spend the time understanding your target audience, you can increase your value with that group faster with the appropriate content strategy.

The bad news is that further splintering of social media channels can lead to smaller audiences over time. For you to optimize your reach and value, the faster you start the personal branding process, the more opportunities you will have to reach a broader audience around the world.

The top 20 social media channels summarized in this book are a place to start while here are some key questions to consider when selecting your channels:

o Do you want your brand to be based on highly visual content or text-based or both?

o Do you want a regional, continental or global brand?

o Which channels best fit your personal and professional strengths and weaknesses and leverage your Unique Selling Propositions?

o Which are your current customers now and what platform(s) do they frequent?

o How do you envision making money with your personal brand in the future and which platform supports that aspiration?

o Are free social media channels the only options to get started or can you invest in a few to optimize content value?

o How much time can you dedicate to building a personal brand and which channels optimize your schedule?

Selecting a primary channel and one or two secondary channels is your next most important decision. Primary and secondary channels are where you deliver *consistent* content in a formulaic approach. You can, as I did, explore opportunistic options to expand the value of your brand on an experimental basis.

More good news is that whatever channel you do select, it will have statistical data to help you measure your personal brand performance. Spend time learning the value of the performance data provided in your targeted channels to continuously improve your content.

As a personal example of this, I monitor the statistics on my primary channel LinkedIn weekly. This includes my content performance in terms of impressions which are averaging nearly 1.3 million per year and my engagements with my audience which were up over 1,700% in the 12 months ending August 2023. LinkedIn also tracks your total followers, profile views, and search appearances.

To clarify:

1. Clean up your current content that does not reflect what you want your brand to stand for.

2. Map out your channel strategy to introduce your personal more valuable brand to the world.

3. Measure and adjust content based on the metrics provided by the platforms that you selected.

Because of social media, we are evolving into a world where everyone can be a micro influencer and monetize a personal brand. As the research outlined in this chapter points out, micro influencers are already more important than celebrities. The faster you elevate the value of your personal brand, the more value you will generate, and the greater your audience will increase.

SUMMARY

o What you must realize is that whatever you share on social media is a manifestation of what you stand for.

o If you want to sell anything, social media is where you need to be.

o If you want to be found online, you need to be on social media.

o There is no better time than the present to differentiate yourself and elevate the value of your personal and professional brand. The advent of social media along with global connectivity through the internet means there is an audience out there waiting to leverage your Unique Selling Propositions for mutual improvement.

o Success evolves out of experimentation. You can and should use additional social media channels to test new ideas or thought leadership concepts. Think of it as a science experiment where you have a hypothesis and undergo multiple tests to prove its validity. Like the Silicon Valley successful business model, fast failure, learning from the experience and taking the lessons learned to improvement is your ultimate goal to maintaining and improving your personal brand.

o The critical first step is having the fire within you to create a future that is fully under your control. The follow up action is to select the appropriate channels to introduce the world to your new and value improved personality.

o Social media is today's magic key to telling your story on your own terms. Selecting a primary channel and one or two secondary channels is your next most important decision.

o Clean up your current content that does not reflect what you want your brand to stand for. Map out your channel strategy to introduce your personal, more valuable, brand to the world. Measure and adjust content based on the metrics provided by the platforms that you selected.

o The faster you elevate the value of your personal brand, the more value you will generate and the greater will audience will increase.

REFLECTIONS

WHEN WAS THE LAST TIME YOU UPDATED
YOUR SOCIAL MEDIA PROFILES?

ARE YOU COMFORTABLE WITH WHAT YOU
ARE POSTING ONLINE?

WHY DID YOU CHOOSE THE PARTICULAR
SOCIAL MEDIA CHANNEL THAT YOU ARE
CURRENTLY USING?

CAN YOU VISUALIZE HOW TO ELEVATE
YOUR SOCIAL MEDIA CONTENT USING
LESS WORDS AND MORE PICTURES?

DO YOU WANT TO BE A MICRO INFLUENCER
AND WHAT WOULD THAT MEAN FOR YOU?

CHAPTER 4

LESSONS FROM MEGA HALL OF FAME PERSONAL BRANDS

> 'ALL OUR DREAMS CAN COME TRUE,
> IF WE HAVE THE COURAGE TO PURSUE THEM.'
>
> WALT DISNEY

Are there days when you wish that you were rich and famous, and are even jealous of some celebrity that you follow in terms of what they have accomplished? We all have these feelings and they too often blur the reality of how those individuals actually became mega stars.

It is extremely rare to find an individual that achieved overnight success. In fact, true inspiration can be found when you take the time to assess what are often humble beginnings of your favorite stars and how they actually became celebrities. Always remember that each of us, at a basic level, are equal human beings.

In this chapter, I begin by reaffirming that even for famous people, the determination to never give up is the ultimate key to success. Next, I go deeper into three of my favorite mega personal brands, exploring their beginnings and the adjustments they made along the way on their personal innovation journeys. What made them super rich?

How did they react to that fame? Why tragedy can be an outcome, even to a powerful successful brand. Why your story will continue to be written, long after you are gone.

Remember, this is *my* shortlist. The attributes and preferred individuals you choose for *your* brand should be *your* inspiration.

FAILURE BEFORE SUCCESS

What do the following individuals have in common?

o Steve Jobs
o Walt Disney
o Albert Einstein
o Oprah Winfrey
o Michael Jordan
o The Beatles
o Colonel Sanders of Kentucky Fried Chicken
o Thomas Edison
o Stephen King
o Sir James Dyson
o Steven Spielberg
o Theodor Seuss Geisel
o Vincent Van Gogh
o JK Rowling

The easy answers include: they are all famous; their talents, not social media, elevated their value; each stands alone as a powerful brand; success was across a wide breadth of functions including science, mathematics, politics, sports and other forms of entertainment.

The reality is that every one of these famous people did not live perfect lives. Let's revisit each of these individuals and groups to understand some of their struggles:

- **STEVE JOBS** At age 30, Jobs was devasted after being fired by the company he co-founded, Apple Computer.[1]
- **WALT DISNEY** This entertainment pioneer was fired from a newspaper for 'lacking imagination' and having no original ideas.[1]
- **ALBERT EINSTEIN** EINSTEIN was not able to speak until almost 4 years old and his teachers stated he would 'never amount to much'.[1]
- **OPRAH WINFREY** Early in her career, Winfrey was demoted from her job as a news anchor because she 'wasn't fit for television'.[1]
- **MICHAEL JORDAN** After being cut from his high school basketball team, Jordan went home, locked himself in his room and cried.[1]
- **THE BEATLES** This famous musical group was rejected by Decca Recording Studios because they did not like their sound and 'they have no future in show business'.[1]
- **COLONEL SANDERS OF KENTUCKY FRIED CHICKEN** His chicken recipe was rejected 1,009 times.[2] When he was 65 years old, Colonel Harland Sanders began franchising his chicken business using his $105 monthly Social Security retirement check and KFC was born.[3]
- **THOMAS EDISON** His teachers said he was, 'Too stupid to learn anything'. Edison is one of the greatest innovators of all time, holding 1,093 patents.[2]
- **STEPHEN KING** He began submitting short stories to magazines at age 16 and hung the rejection notes on a hook which he had to replace and make larger multiple times. His first novel *Carrie* was rejected 30 times before it was published.[2]
- **SIR JAMES DYSON** Over 15 years, this inventor went through 5,126 failed prototypes before he perfected the first working Dyson Vacuum Cleaner.[4]

- **STEVEN SPIELBERG** You might not believe that this famous director whose movies have grossed $9 billion was rejected twice as an applicant student by the University of Southern California's School of Cinematic Arts.[4]
- **THEODOR SEUSS GEISEL** Known to many children worldwide as Dr Seuss, his first book was rejected by 27 publishers.[4]
- **VINCENT VAN GOGH** Today you are likely to pay more than $100 million for an original painting, but in his lifetime, Van Gogh only sold one masterpiece and the sale came not long before his death.[4]
- **JK ROWLING** This author was a broke, depressed, divorced single mother writing her first novel while studying.[4] The first *Harry Potter* book was rejected 12 times by publishers.[5]

DETERMINATION BREEDS SUCCESS

There are some important lessons from the above list of individuals that should fuel inspiration for the growth of your personal brand.

Obstacles early in life are actually helpful in shaping our lives and helping identify the true self that is inside each of us. Several of the individuals listed were labeled problem children yet they achieved astronomical success. Cry your pain away as Michael Jordan did, but if you fight hard enough, the inner strength we all have inside will emerge.

Being fired from whatever job you have or, even worse, putting up with a demoralizing work experience, is not a reason to stop searching for what motivates you to succeed. Prove to the world, and your former employer, the valuable skills they will miss. In those moments of dreaming of what could be that dream career, think of Disney and Jobs and how they reacted to job challenges to emerge stronger in the next life adventure.

Failure is not an option. Each of us has unique talents to showcase the world. I shared a wide-ranging list of individuals across various planned careers to illustrate that you have many options on which to build your own custom designed successful brand.

Think of your life as a continuous set of experiments. The more you test, the closer you are to your dreams. As every successful salesperson will tell you, it's playing the odds. In direct sales, the more customer calls you make, the more success you will achieve, and the more money you will earn. The odds are in your favor as long as you never stop continuously improving your capabilities.

Age is just a number. Look at Jobs who, reaching middle age, was fired from his own co-created company. Alternatively, think of Colonel Sanders who found his chicken dream at the age of 65. At any age, you can take masterful life changing steps to astronomical success.

Where would Van Gogh be now with Instagram and other social media visual platforms available to them to showcase their talents? Your market access today is almost endless if you focus on showcasing your talents to the broader audience that is out there.

Today, we think of the people just discussed as famous. Yet, like you and me, they are basic human beings who wake up in the morning, get dressed and go to work. They felt pain and rebounded from rejection. They found their true talent and their tenacity rewarded them with personal and monetary success.

As Mark Twain once said, 'Keep away from people who try to belittle your ambitions. Small people always do that, but the really great make you feel that you, too, can become great.'[6] Look to the many examples around you, including the ones in this book for the great people to inspire your own valuable personal branding journey.

THE VIRGIN ENTREPRENEUR

My first example of a favorite mega personal brand with a fascinating career is Richard Branson. As of June 2023, according to *Forbes*, Branson has a net worth of over $3 billion USD.[7]

In the days before social media, how did Richard Branson create a personal brand? What were the catalysts that drove his success? How does he continue to build his brand?

To set the scene in terms of why he is a favorite brand, here is how Branson summarized his profile on X (formerly Twitter) in June 2023. 'Tie-loathing adventurer, philanthropist & troublemaker, who believes in turning ideas into reality. Astronaut 001, otherwise known as Dr Yes at Virgin.'[8]

Richard Charles Nicholas Branson was born on July 18, 1950 in Surrey, England to a barrister father and flight attendant mother.[9]

Struggling with dyslexia, Richard failed at multiple schools before dropping out at age 16 to start a youth culture magazine called *Student*. Launched in 1966 and run by students, the first edition sold $8,000 worth of advertising which covered the cost of the first 50,000 copies which were given away free.[10]

In 1969, Branson moved to a London commune surrounded by the British music and drug scene.[11] In 1970 with his friend Nik Powell, Branson launched a mail order record business which they called Virgin, because they were entirely new to the business.[12] The company did well enough that Branson decided to open a record shop on Oxford Street, London and with the increased income opened a recording studio in 1972 in Oxfordshire, England. The first artist to record on the label was Mike Oldfield and his single *Tubular Bells* in 1973 stayed in the UK music charts for 247 weeks.[13]

Never wanting to stand still, in 1980 Branson launched the Voyager Group travel company, the Virgin Atlantic airline in 1984, and a series of Virgin megastores. Struggling to make a profit, in 1992 Virgin Records was sold to Thorn EMI for $1 billion.[14]

Wanting to stay in the music business, Virgin Radio was launched in 1993 and in 1996 a second record company, V2, was created. The Virgin Group eventually expanded into 35 countries and included a train company, a luxury game preserve, a mobile phone company and the space-tourism company, Virgin Galactic.[15]

As his X profile illustrates, Branson is a showman who likes to have fun. His many stunts include: trying to fly around the world in a hot air balloon; wearing a wedding dress to publicize his Virgin Brides retail store; driving a tank down Fifth Avenue in New York City; celebrating his first Virgin America flight by bungee jumping off the Palms Hotel and Casino in Las Vegas; after losing a Formula 1 bet with the CEO of Air Asia airline, dressing as a female flight attendant for that airline; wearing a tuxedo while driving across the English Channel in an amphibious car; posing as Elvis with showgirls in Las Vegas to commemorate flights to that city; and wearing a spacesuit to Virgin Galactic's press conference.[16]

Sir Richard Branson was knighted by Queen Elizabeth II on March 20, 2000 for services to entrepreneurship.[17] He earned his first million dollars back in 1973 at age 23 and entered the billionaire club two decades later at age 41.[18] On social media, he currently has over 40 million followers and he 'blogs regularly on issues ranging from entrepreneurship to the environment and adventure to purpose'.[19]

TURN BIG DREAMS INTO EVEN BIGGER
REWARDING REALITIES

There is a reason I selected Richard Branson as my first example of a brand value champion. On Linkedin, the leading channel for my social media activities, he is number two in terms of followers with nearly 20 million people (number one is Bill Gates with nearly 36 million followers).[20]

I also have a dyslexic son who struggled early in his life and, coincidentally, Branson has the same issue. As this image from Branson's LinkedIn profile clearly illustrates, he is not afraid to embrace this learning disability.[21]

Richard Branson · 3rd
Founder at Virgin Group

Virgin Group

Stowe School

Top Voice

Talks about #travel, #virginfamily, #sustainability, #dyslexicthinking, and #entrepreneurship

Contact info

19,801,918 followers

We were lucky enough to identify dyslexia early in my son's life and put in place aggressive remedial enhanced educational steps to help him become the positive individual he is today. Like Branson, my son is now an ardent adventurer, caring about the environment and exploring ways to improve humanity.

A few of the many other famous dyslexics include Mohammad Ali, Charles Schwab, Henry Ford, William Hewett, Thomas Edison, Tommy Hilfiger, George Patton, George Washington, John Lennon, Albert Einstein, Michael Faraday, Steven Spielberg, Andy Warhol, Leonardo Da Vinci, Pablo Picasso, Agatha Christie, F Scott Fitzgerald, and Hans Christian Andersen.[22] All these individuals turned their learning disability 'disadvantages' into their strengths in finding alternate and creative approaches to solve problems and overcome difficulties.

Dyslexia was not going to stop Branson from turning his big dreams into realities. As blogger Swati Joshi best summarized, 'Richard Branson, the billionaire business magnate, is the poster (boy) of modern personal branding. He is a shining example of what a well-nurtured personal brand can do for your professional fortunes. He is neither highly educated (a school dropout at the age of 16) nor comes from a wealthy lineage. He did badly in school and nobody knew what to make of him. His success has all boiled down to his resourcefulness, dare-devil spirit and understanding of personal branding.'[23]

Joshi highlights several major traits that reflect the Richard Branson personal brand:[24]

He projects an infectious, congenial, fun, bold, adventurous personality which are reinforced with the many publicity stunts that he incorporates into each new venture launched.

1. He is seen as a champion of disruptive innovation, taking on slow moving companies across multiple industries where customer service requires improvement.
2. He encourages young people to start new companies, is involved in a variety of startup events, and even funds them. He is recognized as a mentor, philanthropist and youth champion.
3. He is open in sharing ideas through books, videos and blogs and is a master in creating content that connects at a personal level with individuals.

As Branson wrote in his book, *Business Stripped Bare: Adventures of a Global Entrepreneur*, whatever you 'decide your new brand will stand for, deliver on that promise. That's the only way you'll ever control your brand. And beware: brands always mean something. If you don't define what the brand means, your competitors will.'[25]

Learning disabilities did not stop Branson from over achieving on his dreams. What is stopping you?

TRANSFORM THE IMPOSSIBLE INTO THE POSSIBLE

My second example of a favorite and fascinating mega personal brand is Elon Musk. As of July 2023, according to Forbes, Musk has a net worth of nearly $249 billion, ranking him the richest individual in the world.[26]

What is Elon Musk's background? In which businesses has he invested? What drives his personal brand?

Lots of books are available and continue to be written on the phenomenon that is Elon Musk. This is not one of them. Our focus is on his personal branding style and how it has evolved over time.

The eldest of three children, Elon Musk was born on June 28, 1971 in Pretoria, South Africa. His father, an engineer, was from South Africa and his mother, a model and nutritionist, was originally from Canada.[27 & 28]

At age 10, Musk was already displaying an interest in both technology and being an entrepreneur. After he became acquainted with a programming code using a Commodore VIC-20 computer, he created a video game called Blastar (similar to Space Invaders) which he later sold to a PC magazine for $500.[29]

Seeking better opportunities than those available in South Africa, at age 17, Musk moved to Canada to attend Queen's University in Kingston, Ontario. Two years later, he transferred to the University of Pennsylvania where he graduated with two degrees: Bachelor of Science in physics; Bachelor of Arts in economics from the Wharton School.[30]

Physics was the greater of the pull and at age 24 he moved to California in the United States to pursue a degree in applied physics from Stanford University. 'Physics is a good framework for thinking. Boil things down to their fundamental truths and reason up from there.'[31]

However, Musk dropped out of the physics program at Stanford in Silicon Valley after just a couple of days because, at 24 years old, he saw major entrepreneurial opportunities all around him with the explosive growth of the internet.[32]

In 1995, with $15,000 and his younger brother Kimball, Musk started Zip2, a web software company to help newspapers develop online guides. In 1999, Zip2 was acquired by Compaq Computer for $341 million.[33]

Musk used the Zip2 buyout money to create X.co, a fintech company, which later merged with a money transfer company called Confinity. The resulting merged companies came to be known as PayPal. Peter Thiel ousted Musk as PayPal CEO before eBay acquired the payments company for $1.5 billion.[34]

From Musk's 11.7% share of PayPal, he profited $180 million. In a 2018 interview, Musk stated that he put $100 million into SpaceX, $70 million into Tesla, and $10 million into SolarCity. 'And I literally had to borrow money for rent.'[35]

Today, Musk's main business ventures are:[36]

- o **SPACEX** A space exploration company with core focus on reusable rockets, space tourism, and satellites for improved internet connectivity. The company recently won a $2.9 billion NASA contract to develop a system for landing astronauts on the moon.

- o **TESLA** A vertically integrated company that manufacturers electric vehicles, a Gigafactory which produces battery packs and stationary systems for those cars, and its own physical / online stores for sale of the finished products. As of April 2023, Tesla has sold 4,061,776 electric vehicles.[37]

- o **OPENAI** Originally a non-profit artificial intelligence research lab with a stated goal of creating artificial intelligence that benefits humanity. In 2019, OpenAI transitioned to a for-profit company and soon partnered with Microsoft after securing $1 billion in investment funding.

- o **THE BORING COMPANY** The idea resulted from being stuck in traffic in Los Angeles. The company wants to construct underground tunnels that allow for faster speed between destinations.

- o **NEURALINK** Founded in 2016, the company employs neuroscientists with the objective to develop implantable brain machine interfaces (BMIs), especially for those with paralysis.

- o **X (FORMERLY TWITTER)** In 2022, Musk acquired X which makes money through advertising and licensing. In 2021, X generated $4.5 billion from advertising and $570 from data licensing, but lost $221 million.

When you crystallize Elon Musk into a few words, he is a visionary and an inventor. He enjoys pushing boundaries to make the impossible ultimately become possible.

BECOME A PATHOLOGICAL OPTIMIST

On Tesla's Investor's Day 2023, Musk uttered the words that explain why he is one of my top favorite mega personal brands. 'I guess I have somewhat of a pathological optimism. Who would try to do this (grow Tesla into an electric car leader and rockets), if they weren't pathologically optimistic?'[38]

The famous Berkshire Hathaway's investors Warren Buffett and Charlie Munger praised Musk's singular vision at their own annual shareholder meeting in May 2023. 'It's the dedication to solving the impossible and every now and then, he'll (Musk) do it. He would not have achieved what he has in life if he hadn't tried for unreasonably extreme objectives.'[39]

Musk's life, like Branson's, is filled with experimentation across multiple industries, always looking to deliver an exceptional experience that invites passionate consumers to join them on a journey of discovery.

You are different from everyone else around you. There is no such thing as a perfect human. Your differences are what make you valuable, especially when you fashion them into a powerful personal brand.

Your mission should never be just about you. Think of Musk and his greater mission to improve humanity. In that broader mission – helping others – is where you will effectively monetize your brand.

All of you would have seen videos of the exploding 'reusable' SpaceX rockets in the early days or the heavily reported news on Tesla production problems. These failures did not destroy the Musk brand. They were necessary steps to improve the products to their next level.

Controversy has also followed Musk on X where, as of August 2023, he had nearly 155 million followers.[40] His stated goal, at that time, was to turn this social media site into a digital global open conversation public square and the world's most accurate real-time information source.

The ardent spirit of optimism that lives in Musk can be inside all of us with the right continuous learning fueling system that is accessible through books and the internet. As the Dalai Lama said, 'Optimism doesn't mean that you are blind to the reality of the situation. It means that you remain motivated to seek a solution to whatever problems arise.'[41]

One of my favorite motivational videos of all time is the 2005 Stanford Commencement Address delivered by Steve Jobs. His conclusion was, 'Your time is limited, so don't waste it living someone else's life. Don't be trapped by dogma – which is living with the results of other people's thinking. Don't let the noise of others' opinions drown out your inner voice. And most important, have the courage to follow your head and intuition. They somehow already know what you truly want to become. Everything else is secondary. Stay Hungry. Stay Foolish.'[42]

THE KING OF BRANDING

The first two mega personal brand examples in this chapter are individuals still living and exploring opportunities to reinvent continuously their personal innovation journey. Note the trend in both having achieved riches, but not satisfied in their constant search for other possibilities to continue to reinforce who they are and their message – their brand.

For my last mega brand example, I debated heavily between two individuals: Steve Jobs and Elvis Presley. What I was seeking was an individual that achieved amazing success, but their life was cut short before really enjoying the fruit of their labor. As you can probably guess by the title of this section, I settled for the 'King of Rock-n-Roll', Elvis Presley.[43]

Elvis Aaron Presley was born in January 1935 in Tupelo, Mississippi, to Vernon (a farmer) and Gladys (a garment worker) Presley.[44] His twin brother, Jesse, was stillborn, leaving Elvis as an only child.[45]

Due to the Great Depression in the United States, Elvis grew up poor as both of his parents struggled to maintain a living wage. Life was not easy in their small two room shotgun house (single story home, one room wide – typically 12 feet / 3.5 meters wide – and two rooms deep without a hallway).[46]

When he was 10 years old, Elvis placed fifth in a talent contest at the Alabama-Mississippi State Fair and for his birthday that year his mother bought him his first guitar. He took guitar lessons for a few years, but was too shy to sing in public.[47]

In 1948 when Elvis was in his early teens, the family moved to Memphis, Tennessee where his love for music blossomed. Singing gospel music is what Elvis credited for his taste in music and for his specific sound. His musical influences also included pop, country and R&B.[48]

After graduating from high school in 1953, Elvis began his full music career with Sun Records in Memphis. A year later his contract was sold to RCA Victor.[49]

In 1955, Elvis became a regular on the KSLA-TV *Louisiana Hayride* television series and it is here where his legendary 'leg-shake' dancing moves became popular. With the release of his first big hit, *Heartbreak Hotel*, Elvis' popularity soared. The following year, 60 million people tuned in to watch him perform on *The Ed Sullivan Show*. As his dancing was deemed provocative for the time, he was shown on television only from the waist up. His music also sparked debates about racial and other social issues.[50]

Elvis was drafted into the United States Army in 1958. That same eventful year, his mother passed away which was a devastating personal setback as they had had a close relationship. In his short two year stint in the army, while stationed in Germany, he met his future wife, Priscilla Beaulieu at a military party.[51]

As a musical performer, Elvis had a successful career with 149 songs appearing in Billboard's Hot 100 Pop Charts in the US. Of these, 114 were in the top 40, 40 were in the top 10, and 18 became numbers ones which spent 80 weeks at the top of the charts. It is estimated that more than 1 billion Elvis records have been sold worldwide.[52]

Elvis also appeared in 31 featured movies and two theatrically released concert documentary films. For a number of years, he was one of Hollywood's top stars and one of its highest paid actors.[53]

By the mid 1970s, however, Elvis was in declining mental health. He divorced Priscilla in 1973 and developed a dangerous addiction to prescription drugs. 'He was addicted to junk food and gained considerable weight. In the last two years of his life, he made erratic stage appearances and lived nearly as a recluse. On the afternoon of August 16 1977, he was found unconscious in his Graceland mansion and rushed to hospital where he has pronounced dead.'[54] He was 42 years old.

WE ALL HAVE A LOT OF LIVING TO DO

The biopic movie *Elvis*,[55] released in 2022, starring Tom Hanks, Austin Butler and Olivia DeJonge, is the reason Elvis Presley was chosen as my third mega personal brand. As my wife will attest, I left that movie extremely angry. Resonating in my mind was the tragic evolution of Elvis' life and the self-inflicted health difficulties that led to his death at such a young age. More importantly, it reminded me that while I consider myself to be still in my prime in terms of my career, time is moving a lot quicker and there is, indeed, a lot more living to do.

Got a Lot o' Livin' To Do is actually a top 40 Elvis Presley hit that he recorded in 1957. In that spirit of continuous improvement towards a legacy defining destination, here are my favorite lessons on personal branding from Elvis Presley.

Similar to Branson and Musk, Elvis' early difficult life challenges did not impede reaching his musical dreams. If you are committed to actually achieving your true life objectives, nothing will stand in your way.

It's the little details that build a powerful brand. Think of Elvis' famous 'leg-shake', his hair and his costumes on stage. They incrementally added to the image of the Elvis brand.

Controversy, properly channeled and managed, adds value to branding. In the 1950s, Elvis' leg-shake was considered scandalous. His music challenged social issues.

The people that surround you and support you are critical to how your brand thrives or dies. The movie was a sober reminder that not everyone in your life is there to help you improve. Pick your inner circle carefully and continuously solicit advice on progress.

Fame and wealth can overwhelm reality. Clearly understand what you are seeking. Hire independent advisors while simultaneously keeping an eye on the financial details yourself.

Addictions, no matter what they are, often turn deadly. Your health should always be Number One and it is the only factor that will matter in whether you accomplish your ultimate life objectives.

How old you are is just a number, but one that goes by way too fast. Elvis ultimately lived a short life, one that was filled with fame which, I suggest, he did not enjoy. Focus on what's most important to you and get it done. Leaving a lasting legacy with your personal brand is a great place to start.

In his lifetime Elvis had many nicknames including 'The Hillbilly Cat', 'Elvis the Pelvis', 'The Memphis Flash', 'The King of Rock-n-Roll' or simply 'The King'.[56] Reflecting on the Hans Christian Andersen parable, Elvis, the musical emperor, really had no clothes. As the lessons from that story teach us, 'When a leader surrounds himself with *"yes" men*, it often leads to absurd and embarrassing results. It is far better to surround oneself with honest people who are unafraid to ask questions or point out deficiencies.'[57]

Translating this message to the mission of this book, you are the King of your personal brand. No one else. But you can define it for the world. Every single day, your persona projects an image of what you stand for. The potential to be in the mega personal branding hall of fame is in all of us.

I wish you more success than Richard Branson and Elon Musk and none of the pain that Elvis suffered in his short life. What happens next is totally up to you, for that action determines whether all your dreams do, indeed, come true.

SUMMARY

o Obstacles early in life can be helpful in shaping our lives and helping identify the true self that is inside all of us.

o Keep away from people who try to belittle your ambitions. Small people always do that, but the really great make you feel that you, too, can become great.

o Whatever you decide your new brand will stand for, deliver on that promise. That's the only way you'll ever control your brand. And beware, brands always mean something. If you don't define what your brand means, your competitors will.

o Exceptional experiences created by your brand are what your audience will follow and become passionate about.

o Your differences are what make you valuable, especially when you fashion them into a powerful personal brand.

o Your mission should never be just about you.

o Optimism doesn't mean that you are blind to the reality of the situation. It means that you remain motivated to seek a solution to whatever problems arise.

o It's the little details that build a powerful brand.

o Your health should always be Number One and it is the only factor that will matter in whether you will accomplish your ultimate life objectives.

o You are the King of your personal brand.

REFLECTIONS

WHAT LESSONS DID YOU LEARN FROM
WHAT YOU CONSIDER YOUR BIGGEST
FAILURE TO DATE?

WHEN WAS THE LAST TIME YOU
TOOK THE TIME TO FOCUS ON
IMPROVING YOUR HEALTH?

HOW SOLID IS YOUR NETWORK
OF PEOPLE AROUND YOU IN TERMS OF
PROVIDING HONEST FEEDBACK ON HOW
YOUR LIFE IS EVOLVING?

WHAT IS YOUR DEFINITION OF SUCCESS?
DO YOU HAVE ASPIRATIONS TO BE
A RICHARD BRANSON, ELON MUSK
OR ELVIS PRESLEY?

CHAPTER 5

ORDINARY PEOPLE ACHIEVING INSPIRATIONAL BRANDING SUCCESS

> 'EVERYONE HAS A WILL TO WIN BUT VERY FEW
> HAVE THE WILL TO PREPARE TO WIN.'
> VINCE LOMBARDI

In the last chapter, we met three mega hall of fame personal brands, looked at their backgrounds, and traced their careers to exceptional success. You probably read their biographies skeptically, thinking these individuals likely had better skills or better luck than you will ever have.

However, what should strike you as important are the humble beginnings of each of these mega stars and how, through determination, each achieved exceptional success. And guess what? You have that same potential. Your skills can be continuously improved to add value and improve the world around us.

Life is a special gift. Obstacles we face on our living journey can either freeze us in a world of mediocrity, or they can be periods of time that strengthen our resolve to improve towards achieving our personal best. Success is not guaranteed, but all of us have the opportunity to create a monetizable legacy-enduring personal brand. The alternative is not trying which, at some point in your life, you will regret.

Aspiration to be a mega brand starts with the perspiration in doing the work to actually get started. With the readily available power of social media and the internet, ordinary people are changing the world.

In this chapter, we will explore the concept of mediocrity. We will then present ordinary people from around the world who have leveraged their unique skills to create valuable personal brands.

THE ENEMY OF GREATNESS

In paraphrasing Winston Churchill, Barbara Stanny wrote, 'Mediocrity sees difficulty in every opportunity. Greatness sees opportunity in every difficulty.'[1] The enemy of greatness is mediocrity.

Some of you may argue, 'I am happy in my current state. Why should I add the additional stress of elevating a personal brand and potentially expose myself to disappointing failure?'

Most of us have a fear of change. It takes work to actually deviate from our normal routines. It can be scary. There is no guarantee of a positive result.

Humans are wired for comfort. It is reflected in the foods we eat, the people we spend time with, the entertainment we seek, the home environment that we create.

Entrepreneur motivational speaker and best-selling author Tony Robbins stresses the importance of 'leverage' in overcoming fear to change. 'Leverage is uncovering what's most important in a person to help them make a commitment to making a change.'[2]

Robbins identifies two important precepts about human behavior and change. 'At the most basic level, there are two forces that motivate people to do what they do: the desire to avoid pain or the desire to gain pleasure. This principle is what causes the "yo-yo" pattern in some people: they go back and forth between taking action to create change and losing their drive to take any action at all. Change is never a matter of ability, it's a matter of motivation. If change is a "should," will people change? No. Change has to be not a "should," but a MUST. To access leverage, you must help someone associate massive PAIN to not changing NOW, and massive PLEASURE to changing immediately.'[3]

In different phases of my own life, I have been nervous of unknown outcomes and responded negatively to petty criticisms. I have fallen into the trap of hiding from change.

However, since creating my own successful personal brand, I can attest that change is now my best friend. I guarantee that the greater happiness and opportunities for growth are on the other side of your comfort zone if you learn to associate pain with standing still and outsized pleasure in reaching for your dreams.

Personal brands are a journey of internal discovery of what you can truly become. Undertaking this transformational journey, as the individuals we will meet next have achieved, leads to life changing results.

FROM WINE TO SOCIAL MEDIA PIONEER

Gary Vaynerchuk, or as he is more commonly known on social media, Gary Vee, was born in Belarus which was once part of the Soviet Union. In 1978, at 3 years old, he and his family emigrated to the United States.[4]

Entrepreneurship was in Gary's blood early in his life. At age 7, he set up his first lemonade stand. At 14, his first job was bagging ice at the family vineyard for $2 per hour. Later he sold baseball cards and by the time he graduated from high school, and with much improved sales skills, he earned $7,000 from this venture. Post high school, Vee attended Mount Ida College and graduated with a Bachelor of Arts in 2002.[5]

Vee ran the family business when he finished college. In the late 1990s, he saw the potential of the internet and set out to make his father's firm the first online distributor of alcoholic drinks. Between 1998 and 2003, Vee helped grow the family business to $60 million. In 2006, he took over the family business (previously called Shoppers Discount Liquors) and renamed it the Wine Library. He also created Wine Library TV, and a YouTube channel promoting the business. Five years later this turned into a daily Vee TV show.[6]

His magnetic personality led to appearances on the Ellen DeGeneres and Conan O'Brien's, *Late Night with Conan O'Brien* show which further increased his popularity. In 2009, together with his brother, Vee created VaynerMedia to assist major organizations in achieving similar success.[7]

VaynerMedia attracted major clients such as the USA National Hockey League, PepsiCo, and GE. In a short amount of time, the company grew to employ 800 people. Services provided included paid media strategy, full service design, influencer marketing, e-commerce and in-house consulting.[8]

Strategies leveraged by Vee to deliver his messages include content marketing, influencer marketing and live streaming videos. He also has the ability to recognize emerging technologies.[9]

Across social media, Vee has more than 30 million followers. His podcast, *Gary Vee Audio Experience*, ranks among the top podcasts globally.[10] He is also a 5-time *New York Times* best-selling author and an active public speaker.[10] As of March 2023, his net-worth stands at $200 million.[11]

Neil Patel was born in England in 1985. The family emigrated 2 years later and settled in California. Growing up, Patel was surrounded by entrepreneurs and he soon aspired to be one. He sold CDs and automotive parts before, at age 15, taking on a full-time job at Knott's Berry Farm. After just 3 months, he moved on to selling Kirby vacuum cleaners for Quality Systems.[12]

Realizing that the average American could not afford to buy a $1,600 vacuum cleaner, Patel searched for new opportunities on Monster.com. Instead of finding a job on that platform, he decided to study their business model and then created his own job board called Advice Monkey.[13]

The creation of his own company led to a realization that it needed marketing help. He hired three different marketing firms which failed to deliver the results he wanted. As a result, he learned internet marketing himself. Advice Monkey started to become popular but never succeeded because the site was not set up to take credit cards.[14]

In a Speech 101 class where he explained how search engines work, one of his classmates asked if Patel wanted to consult with Elpac Electronics on their internet marketing strategy. Using the sales skills learned from selling those vacuum cleaners, he convinced them to give him a consulting contract.[15]

Realizing that he could make a lot of money by doing internet marketing, Patel decided to start another company. With the son of the owner of Elpac Electronics, they launched Crazy Egg.[16] This company helps businesses improve their website's usability and conversion rates. With the knowledge from Crazy Egg, Patel also co-founded KISSmetrics, a software company that provides web analytics and customer intelligence solutions.[17]

Today, Patel is a *New York Times* best-selling author, the *Wall Street Journal* calls him a top influencer on the internet,[18] and *Forbes* named him a top 10 marketer.[18] He has worked with companies such as Amazon, Microsoft, Airbnb, Google, Thomson Reuters, Viacom and many more.[18]

Patel's marketing blog generates over 4 million visitors per month, his Marketing School podcast generates over 1 million listens per month, the YouTube channel focused on marketing has over 31 million views and more than 750,000 subscribers, on Facebook there are 1 million fans, and on Twitter over 350,000 followers. He has also spoken at over 300 conferences and companies around the world.[19]

WRITE YOUR WAY TO A PERSONAL BRAND

Carol Tice's love for writing came early. Her pre-teen genre was songwriting. At age 14, she transitioned to essay writing after winning a contest in the *Los Angeles Weekly*. Her regular job was a legal secretary at MGM, the William Morris Agency, and other entertainment companies.[20]

As her writing career grew, Tice wrote extensively for the *Los Angeles Reader* and edited for the alt paper *Random Lengths* in San Pedro, California. She also produced, wrote, and served as on-air talent on Pacifica Radio Station KPFK Los Angeles 90.7 FM.[21]

Tice attended UC Santa Barbara and studied journalism through the UCLA extension. Although born in Los Angeles, she eventually moved to Seattle where she currently resides.[22]

In Seattle, her career included as she put it, 'Five glamorous years' traveling and covering home improvement retailing for the publication national *Home Center News*. This was followed by 7 years as a staff writer at the *Puget Sound Business Journal*, writing four stories per week.[23]

Tice was ultimately fired from her last writing position in Seattle after a new editor took over the business weekly. She switched to freelancing and within 6 months adopted this as her permanent position. She enjoyed the schedule freedom from freelance work, especially after adopting two special-needs children.[24]

To get the word out on her freelance capabilities, Tice leveraged her personal website and the LinkedIn social media platform. LinkedIn landed her four different Fortune 500 clients when they approached her.[25]

As Tice said, 'LinkedIn is the phone book for hiring freelancers in the eyes of large corporations. They're constantly doing searches on LinkedIn and looking at profiles. I really like using In-Mail as well. You can look at who's viewed your profile on Linkedin, then send them an In-Mail email and say, "Hey, are you looking for a writer? I saw you were checking out my profile. Let me know if I can help with anything. I know your industry."'[26]

Just as important for Tice was keeping her writer website and LinkedIn profile continuously updated and making sure it contained key words that were optimized for search engines. She searched for 'Seattle freelance writer' and checked out who surfaced on the search engine and then worked to elevate her presence in the rankings.[27]

Tice's website and LinkedIn became important tools in building a personal brand around freelance writing. Over the years, she increased the value of her brands through a full library of books and e-books focused on freelancing.[28] Additionally, she created two websites (Make a Living Writing Blog and Freelance Writing Den) that help freelance writers earn more through free information, paid courses and community outreach.[29]

Across all the websites and social media channels, Tice uses the same headshots. Her message is also consistent in her copy. It focuses on her skills and provides proof of the ways she can help other writers.[30]

Success followed with her blog makealivingwriting.com growing to 1 million annual readers and 2.5 million readers engaging with her content on *Forbes*.[31] Clients have included Shopify, Costco, American

Express, Dun & Bradstreet, Deloitte, Entrepreneur, Delta Sky magazine and many more. Tice has also helped 15,000+ writers earn more and build independent home-based businesses.[31]

BLOG YOUR WAY TO RICHES

Adam Enfroy was born on September 11, 1987 in Southfield, Michigan. In his personal profile, Enfroy writes on being bullied in grade school, doing well in high school, being kicked out of university for partying too much, and moving back home to live with his parents for a 6 month sentence that kicked him in the behind. It was in that half year distraction-free period at home that he discovered digital marketing.[32]

To escape his problems, he started helping others with digital marketing – SEO, PPC, email marketing, social media, web development – and anything else that people requested. He returned to university, finished the remaining classes to graduate, while still teaching himself digital marketing and helping others.[33]

At age 25, he started making some money as a digital marketing consultant while living with his brother in Michigan, but still struggled to find a full-time salaried position in marketing. A 3-day personal development seminar is what Enfroy credits as changing his life forever. The intensive sessions focused on details of personal life, delving into how our human minds operate in the modern world.[34]

As those 3 profound days came to end, Enfroy began to understand his deepest feelings:[35]

o Getting bullied as a child was still affecting his self-worth as an adult.

o Fear of rejection was holding him back from taking risks.

o The meaning we put behind other people's actions is a human-made concept and unique to every person – it does not physically exist in reality.

o The past cannot be changed and the future is unknown. What matters is now.

o The human mind has infinite untapped potential and the only thing in its way is you.

o Enfroy left that seminar on fire with ideas but did not act on them until 2018 when he decided to leave Michigan and accept a digital marketing position in Texas. At his new company, he was tasked to aggressively recruit, activate, and engage bloggers and influencers to promote his company.[36]

Seeing affiliates making major money from their blog content sparked intensive curiosity. After growing the company's affiliate program and generating Monthly Recurring Revenue (MRR), Enfroy was promoted and became Head of Digital Marketing, managing a team and a $10+ million advertising budget.[37]

In late 2018, Enfroy realized, 'Whether I live in a prison of my creation or enjoy a life of abundance, it's a daily choice only I can make. Not my employer. Not society. Not my past. Not my parents. Only me.'[38] For 6 months he worked 100+ hours per week both on his corporate job and on his own personal blog.[39]

Enfroy's success in blogging came from focusing on growth tactics and treating the work as a side business that he wanted to monetize in less than a year. Instead of taking the typical route of writing, promoting and sharing content, he put his entire focus on the scaling processes.[40]

The processes that he selected had three primary goals: obtain backlinks to build domain authority; accelerate organic traffic growth; and monetize site within 3-6 months. Enfroy's SEO skills that he used to update content elevated his articles in Google search engines. Once his posts reached page 1 on Google, he added affiliate links and started monetizing them.[41]

Three months into this process, Enfroy obtained 500 backlinks and generated 7,600 organic visitors per month. Six months in, backlinks rose to 3,000 and organic traffic increased to 44,000 visitors per month. His blog was now making him more money that his full-time job. Nine months in, the blog was making $35,000 per month; in February 2020 it reached $45,000 per month, and finally in May 2020, $80,000 per month. At age 31, it was time to quit the corporate world and focus entirely on his blog.[42]

Enfroy has been featured in *Forbes*, *Entrepreneur*, *Business Insider*, Yahoo Finance, and US News & World Report. He grew his website from 0 to 500,000 monthly visitors and a 7-figure in revenue in under 2 years.[43] As of November 2022, his net worth stood at $12 million.[44]

TIME FOR SOME MICRO BRANDING INSPIRATION

Vaynerchuk, Tice and Enfroy are inspirational in terms of how they got started on their branding journey, the audience they built and the monetary rewards they are reaping. You might be thinking, that is too much hard work to reach these levels. But building a personal brand is a journey and what you need to realize is that there is incremental value you can monetize along the way.

Let's now look deeper into micro influencers which again is the level with a follower count range between 10,000 and 100,000.

Micro influencers have 22.2 times more weekly conversations that include product recommendations when compared to an average consumer.[45] Top influencers in this category have substantial impact on customer behavior; 63% of consumers consider nano and micro influencers to be more trustworthy compared to the macro and mega influencers.[46] Because of their highly concentrated personal branding focusing on typically one topic, micro influencers are seen as having more knowledge and passion which typically translates to higher engagement and conversion rates.

An example Instagram micro influencer is Alina Gavrilow, a New York-based lawyer turned fashion blogger. To her roughly 100,000 followers, she calls herself the 'Blazer Queen' and showcases classic and feminine style and 9-to-5 outfits for young working women.[47] In 2014, Gavrilow launched her own The Closet Crush personal website for daily feminine style inspiration where she invites followers to shop her styles on Instagram.[48]

If beauty is your category, then meet multi-awarded and beauty journalist Eleanor Pendleton, one of the top micro influencers on Instagram in 2022.[49] Again, with roughly 100,000 followers, her personal brand evolved to launching *Gritty Pretty*, Australia's leading online beauty publication that covers all things beauty, fashion, and interior inspiration.[50]

If you enjoy traveling, then meet micro influencer Francesca Newman-Young (approximately 85,000 Instagram followers) who is a full-time blogger, *Huffington Post* contributor, and brand consultant from South West London.[51] On her successful personal blog, she writes about her love for travel, fashion and lifestyle.[52]

Food and eating healthy may be your passion. If this is the case, then meet micro influencer Lindsay Cotter(86,000 Instagram followers) who focuses on sports nutrition and gluten-free diets.[53] Motivated by her husband who is a former triathlete, in 2009 Cotter created Cotter Crunch, a nutrition resource for athletes and she added gluten-free to help combat her own health problems.[54]

Technology is my passion and in researching this book, I came across Hitesh Kumar (just over 95,000 Instagram followers) who is one of India's top micro influencers in tech and gaming.[55] He has an amazing 2+ million subscribers on YouTube where he provides information on new gadgets, games, and technical devices.[56]

IF NOT MICRO, MAYBE NANO

Individual nano influencers have a follower count of 1,000 to 10,000. This level of personal brands, with fewer followers, have 7 times the engagement rate than mega influencers.[57] The smaller audience is an advantage as there is a deeper connection to the topic bringing the group together.

An example nano influencer is Chantelle Coustol, a Texas-based Canadian mom influencer and wellness advocate with just over 10,000 Instagram followers.[58] She is a Platinum member of Young Living (YL) Essential Oils and a distributor of YL products through her wellness business, Petal and Seeds. [59] She also has a YouTube channel with over 9,000 subscribers.[60]

Another nano influencer example is Jeriel Melgarez (just over 9,000 Instagram followers) who is Honduras-born, now living in Tampa, Florida who focuses on fashion and lifestyle. He showcases his style on Instagram and has collaborated with brands like 1017 ALYX 9SM and Every Man Jack.[61]

In Chapter 7 I will revisit this aspect of our Influencer world, delving further into the various levels of brand creation but for now let's focus in more detail on how individual success stories can motivate *you*.

INSPIRATION SUCCESS AT EVERY LEVEL

In the last chapter we met mega influencers Richard Branson, Elon Musk and Elvis Presley. Their inspirational journey to being celebrities may have seemed daunting as you think about crafting your own personal branding journey. Yet in this chapter we have seen how average individuals have differentiated themselves by crafting unique personal brands that elevated and monetized their value. Terms like macro, micro, and nano are just words. The message is really in the stories you read of ordinary people who decided at some point in their lives to take the leap into publicly expressing their passions. Those same feelings and possibilities to make positive, forever, legacy fulfilling changes are in each of us.

Gary Vaynerchuk was born into a family business, but he had a deeper fire in him to build a media company that he successfully evolved into a totally new direction. Neil Patel took the art of internet marketing to an amazing revenue growth level.Carol Tice was fired from her corporate writing job and turned that setback into a fulfilling freelancing career. Adam Enfroy was kicked out of college, but he turned his life around and through digital marketing elevated blogging to a profitable business.

The common denominator to Vaynerchuk, Tice, and Enfroy was the internet and social media. These digital tools allowed them to reach broad audiences and monetize their brands. Consistency and keeping their sites updated, including focusing on how Google managed their content, is partly what made them successful.

Micro influencers Alina Gavrilow, Eleanor Pendleton, Francesca Newman-Young, Lindsay Cotter, and Hitesh Kumar ideated their passions into a personal brand. Note that the examples for each of these are across business types such as fashion, beauty, travel, food or technology.

Nano influencers Chantelle Coustol and Jeriel Melgarez confirm that you do not need to over think the size of your audience to get started. You can, with the correct strategy, build and monetize a personal brand at multiple levels. Your value increases as the size of the audience increases. Key is taking action by creating a formula such as what is described in this book that fits your personality.

Note the variety of countries represented by these ordinary people in launching their personal brand. It is not where you start or the circumstances that you fall under. No matter where you are in the world, in you are possibilities for extraordinary success.

THE WILL TO WIN

A successful personal brand requires consistent feeding of valuable content to grow your audience. The individuals identified in this chapter are on a journey of advancement which may change over time. As you research them after reading this book, they may have taken their brand in a different direction. That same choice is available to you on your personal journey as you explore the possibilities of elevating your value to the world. Start and adjust as you see either changes in your priorities or the availability of improved technologies.

Your personal brand is your company, especially when you unveil it publicly to the world. At its core should be your skills and your determination to continuously improve them. Think carefully about the formula; research other individuals that are ahead of you; and on a regular basis engage your audience for feedback on your activities.

Take a look again at Vince Lombardi's quote at the beginning of this chapter. We may not express it overtly, but we all have a will to win. To achieve your true potential, you need to put in the time and the work to prepare to win.

Ordinary people can achieve exceptional life outcomes. If you are reading this book and following its lessons, you have the will to win and are destined for greatness. It is now time to prepare to win.

SUMMARY

o Aspiration to be a mega brand starts with the perspiration in doing the work to get started.

o Life is a special gift. Obstacles we face on that living journey can either freeze us in a world of mediocrity, or they can be periods of time that strengthen our resolve to improve towards achieving our personal best.

o Success is not guaranteed, but not trying to achieve something so unique that it leaves a lasting legacy long after you're gone will be your biggest regret.

o Change is your best friend, especially when you live in a world of accelerated technology adoption.

o The human mind has infinite untapped potential and the only thing in its way is you.

o The feelings and possibilities to make positive forever legacy fulfilling changes are in each of us.

o A successful personal brand requires consistent feeding of valuable content to grow your audience.

o Your personal brand is your company, especially when you unveil it publicly to the world.

REFLECTIONS

WHICH OF YOUR CORE
PASSIONS CAN BE ELEVATED
TO A PERSONAL BRAND?

WHERE ARE YOU INVESTING
YOUR FREE TIME TODAY?

WHAT DO YOU CONSIDER
IS A LONG WORKING DAY
AND HOW DOES IT COMPARE
TO THE INDIVIDUALS IN
THIS CHAPTER?

WHICH COMPANY DO YOU
CONSIDER GREAT AND WHY?

CHAPTER 6

THE SECRET SUCCESS BRANDING FORMULA

'THE SECRET TO GETTING AHEAD
IS GETTING STARTED.'

MARK TWAIN

On that restless London night when I did not get the big promotion that would have changed my life, I came up with a hypothesis. What if I could create a personal brand and, through a defined formula, showcase it to the world? What experiments could I undertake to test out my brand theory?

The angel on one shoulder versus the devil on the other kept fighting with each other as I tossed and turned trying to crystalize a plan. This idea will take up too much time, said the devil. And, he added, it's probably going to impact your current job performance; you cannot afford to lose your job; you have a family to support; you need to save for retirement; it's going to cost too much money to create a personal brand.

Luckily for me, the angel was stronger, reminding me that at some levels creating a personal brand could be an extension of what I was doing already; there must be technology out there that can automate some of the functions; there must be people already doing this; what could they teach me; there must be ingredients already available that I could introduce to get started.

As ideas to test the hypothesis popped into my head, I turned on the light and scribbled those ideas on a hotel napkin. I do not remember how many times I did this and maybe I did finally fall asleep for a couple of hours, but the following morning I was pleased with more positive than negative notes. I had a plan!

WHERE TO START?

Getting started, after a major tipping point setback, on some levels felt overwhelming. However, looking back, what was comforting was that I firmly believed I had a story to tell around some core themes.

Just as in a scientific experiment, I formulated a hypothesis or theory of how to transform my life. I based that hypothesis on work I was already doing and enjoying. The experiments that would follow were to test out where what I was already doing could be taken to a different personal value enhancing level.

In my first blog back in 2012, the general themes I outlined were:[1]

o   Ideas on leadership, innovation, technology and global retail trends.

o   Interest in mobility, social media, e-commerce, security, global cultures and emerging markets.

When I started, I had more questions than answers. Would I restrict my blog to the retail industry? Would I focus on leadership, innovation and technology which were already my passions? Could this really become a personal brand that attracts an audience?

The inspiration for the next steps came from my daughter's writings. Write about what's important in the moment and make it come alive through your analysis on what it means to you and potentially to those folks that take the time to read the material.[2]

Prophetically, back in 2012, I chose two still-evolving technology trends that would be my focus:[3]

1. **VIDEO** The importance of visual imaging to drive behavior, global collaboration and commerce are dramatically increasing. Think of the success of YouTube where over 3 billion hours of video are watched each month.[3] Future messaging needs to be increasingly visual, high impacting, short, and built to go viral. This is true for a simple advertisement that runs 30 seconds for a retail store or for anyone with an idea they want to turn into a business. The more visually impactful you can state your key message, your business idea and your presentation, the greater the lasting impact on your audience in taking a positive action towards your business goals. Take most of your words out of your PowerPoint presentation. Focus on visuals and intersperse your message with video content. More than words on a page, visual imaging, especially short videos, resonate longer with your audience.

2. **SOCIAL NETWORKING** Is social media a fad? Can it be monetized? What does it mean for industries such as retail? To understand social media, you need to get beyond some of the early models that were focused on what you had for dinner last night and decide what this technology is all about. Social media is a market segmentation evolutionary step. It is a journey just started where audiences that have the same preferences, same complaints, same shopping likes and, yes, even some same diseases, can find each other on common technology ground and have a virtual conversation. Social media creates greater targeted market niches that successful entrepreneurs can explore to build new businesses. All of us have the potential to both drive and profit from the social media journey by understanding the basic themes that drive us and finding our online partners in the 2.1 billion people that will be on the internet by the end of 2012.[3]

It is worth noting the dramatic change since 2012 in the key statistics cited with both video and social networking. In 2012, for YouTube, over 3 billion hours of video were watched each month.[3] In 2023, that number of YouTube views exponentially jumped to a whopping daily figure of 1 billion hours which translates to around 5 billion actual videos consumed, per day.[4]

By the end of 2012, the projections were for 2.1 billion to be on the global internet.[3] As outlined in Chapter 3, the global internet audience has more than doubled to 5.16 billion or 64% of the current global population.[5]

o What are the other key takeaways from my early experiments in creating a personal brand?

o The hypothesis was that I could create a personal brand around what I was already passionate about.

o Mentally, there was a vision on the key themes that could create value for an audience.

o I understood that the mission was to identify channels to deliver the content.

o The inspiration of how to get started was from someone else's writings, reinforcing the idea that I was not alone.

o The solution, built on the knowledge of what I believed at that time, were the two most important growing technologies: video and social media.

My initial formula was not perfect. It was probably too wide in ideas, but it formed the impetus to get started and that is the most important step.

CREATE A PERSONAL BRAND HYPOTHESIS

The *Oxford Learner's Dictionary* defines a hypothesis as an idea or explanation of something that is based on a few known facts but that has not yet been proved to be true or correct.[6] Key words in this definition are: few known facts which need to be proven.

Your personal branding journey needs to begin with a general hypothesis on the core ideas that will define the value you want to showcase to the world which is why Chapter 2 was designed to get you thinking more clearly on what you stand for. This is the ideal place to start.

The following quotes from Ralph Waldo Emerson helped me understand the steps to take next:[7]

- For every minute you are angry you lose 60 seconds of happiness.
- The only person you are destined to become is the person you decide to be.
- You become what you think about all day long.
- Life is a journey, not a destination.

Stop fixating on what you cannot change such as past painful experiences. Focus on what is within you that is unique. Whatever hypothesis you create about you as a brand, think about it and its evolution every single day. You will not have all the answers on day one. You will make mistakes. Personal branding is a value adding journey whose destination at first you may not fully realize possible.

If you need inspiration to create a hypothesis, re-read Chapter 3. Additionally, research your preferred social media channels for individuals that have effectively monetized their brand to understand their strategy. What value are they projecting? How are they making money from their online presence? If you are stuck, you can even develop a hypothesis on how you can create a variation on the successful individuals that will showcase your own personal brand.

A personal brand hypothesis is a blend of what you stand for that is unique linked to the social media channels that allow you to showcase it. As you begin, the formula for testing your ideas does not need to be perfect. You will discover, as I did, that success is the result of consistency and continuous adjustments until you reach your intended destination.

What is optimal about social media is that it provides tools for constantly checking whether you are on the right track. Your audience response to your leadership ideas is one example. Another which I use sporadically is to get an audience assessment of my formula through surveys in my favorite channels, asking for validation that value is still being delivered by my content.

In essence, create a hypothesis for your personal brand that is a combination of what you stand for and the social media channels that allow you to elevate its value. Begin experiments in those social media channels to test your ideas. Periodically check in with your audience either through engagement or surveys to adjust the journey as necessary.

SUPPORT YOUR BRAND WITH RELEVANT CONTENT

My experience indicates that crafting a personal brand is typically not something you can do while ignoring your current job that is paying the bills. If you are in a corporate role, that role also deserves 100% of your effort to sustain the value of that brand.

Adding a formula to elevate your personal brand to your current position delivers substantial benefits. As you have already read, the companies where I was employed supported my individualistic approach to highlight my brand, but only because I maintained a similar focus on delivering high value at work. In other words, my employee performance did not decrease as I began focusing on my personal brand.

Luckily, I discovered early on in my branding journey that the only way I could sustain high performance in both my current professional position and also showcasing my unique selling propositions was through automation. Timing was on my side as the growing number of apps and online software solutions came to the rescue.

My personal brand is based on delivering content that is generated directly by me, but I also enjoy including in the formula leadership content created by others that thematically supports my ideas. My first approach to finding third party content was simply searching the internet. As this process was tedious and time consuming, I researched and found a major productivity improvement research tool called Flipboard which I still use today. Flipboard's tagline is 'Get Informed, Get Inspired, Stories Curated for You' and it delivers on that promise.[8]

Flipboard is an article consolidator website. The site learns what you are researching on their apps and over time finds and delivers that content directly to you either in summary format or in specific channels that you can add to your Flipboard profile to consolidate content.

Flipboard is extremely user friendly and was an effective tool in finding online content that I could share to enhance my brand. The allure of the mobile app was that in down time or what was previously wasted time, I could research content and store it later for scheduling on my social media channels.

If I was standing in line at the airport waiting to board a flight, if I was traveling on a train, if the television program in front of me was boring, I turned to Flipboard to find content to publish. What I considered unproductive time transitioned into social media research to identify the best content that would reflect my brand.

My approach was to quickly flip through articles of potential interest and when I found one that I liked, I emailed it to myself for later scheduling. We will shortly dig deeper into this critical scheduling part.

Reading third-party content often sparked new ideas to improve my approach to personal branding. Sourcing articles through Flipboard became one of my favorite activities to increase my level of knowledge in the exact themes that increased the value of my brand.

If you are just starting your branding journey or are on one now, news aggregator sites are an invaluable tool to automate the research, support others that are generating important articles, inspire your own content and differentiate your value-added messaging to the world.

OPTIMIZE SCHEDULING OF YOUR CONTENT

Gathering content using news aggregator apps was a major time saver when I started my social media branding odyssey, but it was not enough. Even more important to growing your audience is timing your news releases to the optimal time they will reach your target audience.

This critical timing element has two components:

3. The hour of the day best optimized for your audience.

4. An understanding of how this varies by social media channels and matching your releases to each.

In both scenarios, there are now multiple tools available that automate social media news releases. I currently use SocialBee.com.[9] Their online platform allows me to:

o Manage all social media profiles in one location.

o Use their Canva graphics design tool or Artificial Intelligence assistant.

o Schedule posts ahead of time in a calendar.

o Publish across all social media profiles.

o Gain insights via analytics on social media performance.

Full disclosure – for a long time I used another industry leading platform but was disappointed in the number of failures to post plus dramatically increased costs. I am paying roughly one third of the cost of the other solution and the performance is much improved.

Lots of choices are available for scheduling content and if you only select one social media channel, some of them even provide this functionality built into their product. Most of the social media scheduling platforms offer a free testing period which I highly recommend. Leverage their training tools and webinars to get productive quickly. Most critically, test their customer service response. The other company that I used for a long time was larger, but had poor customer service.

Timing your content to each social media channel is also important. The best time to post on social media overall is Tuesdays, Wednesdays, Thursdays at 9am to 10am. The same study from Sprout Social found that Wednesday morning is the perfect time to publish on Facebook, Instagram, X (formerly Twitter), and LinkedIn. Sunday is the worst time to post on social media.[10]

By social media channel, here are the recommendation for optimal posting times:[11]

o **FACEBOOK** Monday 11am – 12pm, Tuesday 10am – 3pm, Wednesday 11am – 3pm, Thursday 2pm – 4pm, Friday 1pm – 4pm.
Best days Tuesday and Friday.

o **INSTAGRAM** Monday 11am – 12pm, Tuesday, 10am – 1pm, Wednesday 10am – 1pm, Thursday 10am – 11am, Friday 10am to 11pm.
Best days Tuesday and Wednesday.
Weekends also see increased engagement for this channel.

o **X** Monday 9am – 4pm, Tuesday 9am – 12pm, Wednesday 9am, Thursday 9am – 4pm, Friday 9am.
Best days Wednesday and Thursday.

o **LINKEDIN** Monday 10am, Tuesday 10am – 12pm, Wednesday 3pm, Thursday 9am – 10am, and Friday 11am – 12pm.
Best days Wednesday and Thursday.

o **TIKTOK** Monday 6am – 10am, Tuesday 2am – 9am, Wednesday 7am – 8am, Thursday 9am – 7pm, Friday 1pm – 3pm.
Best days Monday and Sunday.

- **YOUTUBE** Monday 2pm – 4pm, Tuesday 2pm – 4pm, Wednesday 2pm – 4pm, Thursday 12pm – 4pm, Friday, 12pm – 4pm, Saturday 9am – 11pm, Sunday 9am – 11am. **Best days** Thursday and Friday.

- **PINTEREST** Monday 2pm – 4am, Tuesdays 2pm to 4am, Wednesday 2pm – 4am, Thursday 2pm – 4am, Friday 8pm – 11am, Saturday, 8pm – 11am.

An important component to consider with the above recommendation is time zones. If you are on one continent and are trying to grow an audience in another with a substantially different time zone, you need to think carefully about the timing of each news item. In my particular case, Europe is important to my personal brand and I include every day an early morning European timed news item that is internationally focused to reach that audience.

Personally, I am still experimenting with the above recommended scheduling recommendations. In the next section, I will explain the current, much simpler calendar I am using that aligns with both time zones and the corporate roles.

BUILD UP YOUR SOCIAL MEDIA WHILE WORKING

If you are full-time employed and pursuing creating a personal brand on the side, keep in mind your employer will see your increased social media presence. I once had a senior executive of a company in which I was employed ask whether I still worked for them or was I spending all my time publishing online. In other words, who was I really working for?

At first, I was upset that someone was questioning my online activities which I believed were mutually beneficial. I'd spent personal time learning new skills through a personal brand and I was projecting those skills in sharing content that supported company leadership initiatives. I was committed to delivering exceptional performance in both the creation of the personal brand and my corporate role.

However, to mitigate any misunderstandings regarding where I was spending my time, I adopted the following simple social media calendar which, for the most part, I still use today (all USA Eastern Time Zones):

o **MONDAY** 2am International News Items to coincide with Europe early morning time zone; 6:30am news item directly from my own original content which could include a podcast, personal video, blog, news mention, etc; 7:30am top three highest engagement social media posts for the week; 12pm or noon retail related article; 5pm leadership article.

o **TUESDAY** 2am another international article for Europe; 6:30am personal original content; 7:30am important independent industry research; 12pm independent infographic; 5pm leadership article.

o **WEDNESDAY** 2am European targeted article; 6:30am personal original content; 7:30am newsworthy independent YouTube video; 12pm independent retail article; 5pm leadership article.

o **THURSDAY** 2am motivational quote; 6:30am personal original content; 7:30am newsworthy YouTube video; 5pm leadership article.

o **FRIDAY** 2am European targeted article; 6:30am personal original content; 7:30am newsworthy YouTube video; 5pm leadership article.

o **SATURDAY / SUNDAY** 2am European targeted article; 8am newsworthy YouTube video; 10am technology or leadership article; 12pm technology or leadership article; 2pm personal original content; 5pm leadership article.

Note anything interesting about the scheduled times? To minimize confusion and to alleviate any senior leadership concerns where I was spending my time, all social media posts are scheduled:

- Before the typical US workday which begins at 8am.
- 12pm ie lunch time.
- 5pm which is technically the end of the workday in US.

Being responsible, I was now sending the message to my corporate senior leadership that I was not spending time on social media during working hours. Turns out, as my largest and most important audience is on Linkedin, this schedule is actually optimal to when the professionals in this channel access the most content.

My social media calendar did deliver the large audience that I was seeking on LinkedIn. The lesson learned from my experience was that, depending on the brand you are trying to develop, it is important you balance any current corporate role with the best times your audience accesses content on your selected channels.

One other trick that I began early in my social media branding journey is scheduling an entire week of content during the previous weekend, typically on a Saturday or Sunday morning. The attraction of social media calendars is that they do the work, even while you are sleeping. This is valuable if your content has a longer shelf life rather than being news in the moment. Through applications such as Flipboard, content that does not need to be published immediately can be scheduled later to still add value to your brand.

Always remember that nothing is static. Using social media calendars is critical to increasing your productivity and timing the content to when your audience wants to read it. Spend time listening to how your particular audience is responding and, when possible, test new ways to increase engagement.

In later years, when I was able to monetize my brand, I finally hired a social media manager to post in real time. Critical to this step was training the individual to my formula and, initially, checking in often to review the content to ensure it reflected what the audience was expecting from my brand.

A successful personal brand is the result of consistent high value delivery of content. In my decade of doing this, I probably missed posting in the defined schedule less than a dozen times. It does take work, but automation is your best friend to high productivity.

INVEST IN A PERSONAL WEBSITE

My initial attempt at building a brand was through blogging as that was the primary tool available to create an audience. It evolved with the addition of social media as it became mainstream and I aligned with LinkedIn as my primary channel.

As I was creating all this content, I realized that there is one big challenge with social media. There are too many channels and it can be hit and miss whether or not your audience actually sees your content.

This is especially true when you consider the explosion of information. There are 300 million photos uploaded to Facebook every day. Each minute, 300 hours of video are uploaded on YouTube. On WhatsApp 60 billion texts are sent on a daily basis. On Instagram, 95 million new pictures appear per day and 1 billion posts make it on X every week.[12]

Where does one go to consolidate the personal brand journey and still grow an audience? My approach was creating a personal website and I was lucky enough to be able to register my name as the domain.

All my original content, especially articles, plus key weekly favorite third party information, you can find on www.tonydonofrio.com.[13] I had this idea early in my personal branding defined plan and I am currently at Version 5 of its evolution.

The site was created by a third party under my direction in terms of the elements I wanted to showcase. Every year, I review the current version with the third party and make adjustments to stay current, especially in the graphics.

Let's take a look at some of the key components of my personal website, starting with the banner.

Thematically, I introduce myself with a picture, links to all my social media channels, key messaging that I am about 'Visionary / Technology / Leadership' highlighting being an award-winning site plus a global retail influencer, and a motivational quote that changes every week.

For instance, one particular week the quote was from Nelson Mandela who said, 'The greatest glory in living is not in falling, but in rising every time we fall.'[14] Recall that I post a motivational quote every Thursday morning at 2am. Each motivational quote is posted on all social media channels and linked to this location on my website. Included in the social media post is a weblink which is actually an anchor that invites readers to visit my website. I use anchors extensively for key content to link the audience to my personal website.

Note also on the website header the drop-down menu options which include services that I offer, a running list of podcasts that I either cohost or where I am a guest (160+ as of August 2023), videos including my own from my YouTube channel, thought leadership content with favorite industry research / infographics / photos, an 'About Me' which includes my biography and a press page listing all the publications where I have appeared and, finally, a 'Contact Me' section.

The next section of my webpage presents my leadership content.

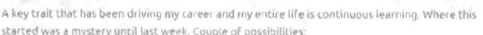

On the left are my chronological original articles or blogs with this particular one being on leadership. Every month, in this section, I publish an original article on the retail industry, technology innovation, or leadership. As the value of my personal brand increased, the same articles are now published on multiple other platforms.

On the right is a 'Sponsored Content' image where I recognize a company or service that is helping monetize my brand. Below it is a graphic representing some of the public speaking stages around the world where I have presented my retail innovation leadership ideas.

Next are the many award badges I continue to receive that support the growth of my personal brand. This includes being named a top 100 Global Retail Influencer in both retail and technology, recognition for my website and my articles. It also includes a couple of the major industry group that I am either on the board of, advisors of, or I support heavily. As you move down the website, you will start to see a pattern.

Why the Physical Store is the Next Profitable Digital Advertising Frontier

Top 3 Weekly Essentials

1. How common are supply chain disruptions?
   Chain Store Age

2. How Bed Bath & Beyond lost its suppliers' trust, and doomed itself
   Retail Dive

3. The resilient leader's 5-point guide to 'make things happen'
   Fast Company

In a previous CEO role, I was on a mission to transition physical security infrastructures into smart highly visual advertising delivery platforms. The rationale is similar to what happening with CCTV video technologies. In 2021, we crossed over 1 billion video cameras installed around the world.

Originally designed as a safety technology to monitor the launch of V-2 rockets in World War II and later taking more prominent roles as security devices, many of today's CCTV cameras are now data gathering eyes. Coupled with Artificial Intelligence and Edge Computing and renamed as

On the left is another original article or blog with this particular one being on retail technology innovation. On the right is an additional link to my YouTube channel.

The top three most popular posts for the week as measured by LinkedIn engagement are below the YouTube link. On the social media calendar, the top three are published on Monday mornings at 7:30am and the link provided is an anchor to my personal website where the reader can access the actual details.

industries including retail.

Look up or the side of shelves in multiple retail formats, and in most modern retail stores you will see yourself on in-store Public View Monitors (PVMs) which were designed to increase visual deterrence against theft. Those same video monitors along with multiple other strategic locations inside the physical store are the perfect location to now add cloud-based digital advertising. Concurrently many of these screens can perform their security functions when needed, but more importantly they can also actually generate revenue for the retail chain through advertising.

PVMs are only the beginning of what is possible with digital advertising inside retail stores. There are multiple other strategic locations, including exits, point-of-sale, self-checkout, in-aisles, end caps, on shelves, etc. where the digital advertising revolution is possible to substantially improve profitability.

The $100+ Billion Retail Media Networks Revenue Opportunity

It is a Small World

"Live Long and Prosper." Spock

Continuing our global journey to learn something new, our next stop is to boldly go, where no one has gone before and learn some fun facts about Star Trek.

In 2016, Star Trek, the original series, celebrated 50 years. Its initial three-year run was not a big success, but syndication in the 1970s turned it into a cult classic. To date, 13 feature films and 12 other television series have followed.

The creator Gene Roddenberry brought into

The Ever Growing Omnipresence of Retail RFID

Continuing our journey down the website, let me share an example of how I have adapted the content to changing times.

On the left again is continuation of my original personal articles on retail technology, February 2023's focus on the growth of RFID for greater inventory visibility in retail.

On the right is an example of a pivot in content taken during the COVID-19 pandemic, called *It's a Small World*. As all travel stopped, I decided to start a series where, using pictures, I would revisit the many places around the world where I have travelled and learned something new about that experience. I always include a relevant quote with each *It's a Small World* post.

This particular picture is from Seattle in the United States where I am sitting in the original chair that was used in the filming of the original *Star Trek* series and which is now located in a museum. The COVID-19 inspired content is published both on Instagram and my personal website. On the social media calendar, the link provided is again an anchor to this website where the reader can learn more, in this case about *Star Trek* and why this was an interesting experience.

Next up are categories and favorite research.

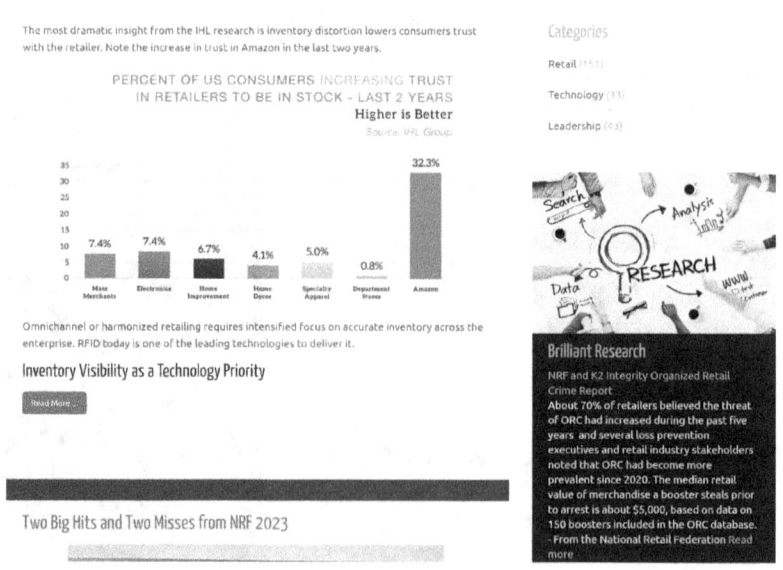

Categories allow readers to access my content via the three major themes that represent my personal brand: retail, technology or innovation, and leadership. As outlined earlier, the focus on these three themes is what drives the Unique Selling Propositions of my personal brand.

Below the categories is my favorite industry research of the week which I title *Brilliant Research*. On the social media calendar, this is posted on Tuesday mornings at 7:30am. The link is again an anchor back to my personal website where the reader can access the content.

By now you must have realized that the left side of the website is reserved for original articles. Continuing with the changing content on the right side, next up are infographics.

The National Retail Federation Big Show this past week in New York did not disappoint. As I summarized in my post NRF 2023 social media post:

"THAT'S A WRAP: An inspiring Retail ROI Super Saturday, an astounding number of NRF 2023 retailer meetings, a roaring 20s Rethink Retail Top 100 influencers bash, hosting the NRF Loss Prevention Council, kicking off LPRC 2023 at Bloomingdale's, named a top 10 NRF original Twitter, on Linked-in 45,000+ impressions / 100%+ engagement, nearly 90,000 steps, launching multiple Prosegur next-gen RFID tech, trend spotting for next article, and most essential FRIENDSHIPS rekindled – it has been an exceptional Retail Innovation Leadership few days. Thank you ALL. "

Appreciative that just prior to the opening of NRF 2023, I was named once again a Top 100 Retail Influencer for 2023 by Rethink Retail. Congratulations to everyone on this important list. Retail needs a broader set of voices more than ever as we transition to a continued disruptive future for the industry.

What were the big hits and misses of the immersive NRF 2023 week? How could the misses

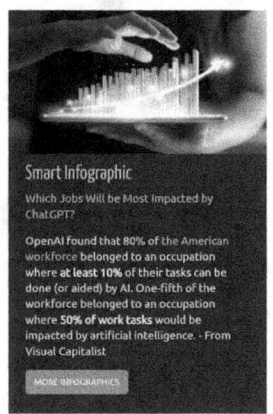

Smart Infographic

Which Jobs Will be Most Impacted by ChatGPT?

OpenAI found that 80% of the American workforce belonged to an occupation where at least 10% of their tasks can be done (or aided) by AI. One-fifth of the workforce belonged to an occupation impacted by artificial intelligence. - From Visual Capitalist

MORE INFOGRAPHICS

Titled *Smart Infographic*, this next section on the right highlights a favorite weekly infographic from a third party. I am a big believer that a picture is worth many words and every week I deliver to my audience a graphical representation of data that again is linked to my three themes representing my brand. As you can see, this particular week it is on the hot topic of ChatGPT.

The final section of the website is again about centralizing content to provide readers with a one stop experience of my brand.

Hit 1: Start with Making a Human Difference to the World

Read More ...

The 2023 Top 5 Strategies and Top 3 Technologies for Retail Success

A cornerstone of my social media growing personal brand has been the continuously updated "Disruptive Future of Retail" presentation that I have delivered on global stages in the past seven years. Crystalizing in the 2022 editions are the five strategies and the three primary technologies that will deliver a more profitable future of retail into the new year.

At the core of these strategies are two stakeholders that hold the key to what happens to retail next: the consumer and the store associate. The smartphone as now the third retail innovation megatrend has re-defined the successful retail formula.

This article summarizes the five strategies for success into 2023, along with the three technologies that are the strategic levers to their successful implementation. It closes with a summary of the smart more profitable store of the future.

The One Chart that Defines the Successful Future of Retail

Read More ...

The Worst is Yet to Come, and for Many 2023 Will Feel Like a Recession

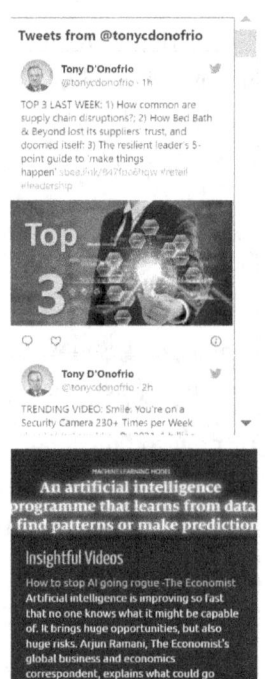

Tweets from @tonycdonofrio

Tony D'Onofrio
@tonycdonofrio · 1h

TOP 3 LAST WEEK: 1) How common are supply chain disruptions?; 2) How Bed Bath & Beyond lost its suppliers' trust, and doomed itself 3) The resilient leader's 5-point guide to 'make things happen' sbee.link/847fcoehqw #retail #leadership

Tony D'Onofrio
@tonycdonofrio · 2h

TRENDING VIDEO: Smile. You're on a Security Camera 230+ Times per Week

An artificial intelligence programme that learns from data find patterns or make prediction

Insightful Videos

How to stop AI going rogue -The Economist Artificial intelligence is improving so fast that no one knows what it might be capable of. It brings huge opportunities, but also huge risks. Arjun Ramani, The Economist's global business and economics correspondent, explains what could go wrong. Read more

On the left is a chronological continuation of my personal articles. On the right is first a duplication of my own live X feeds. As each news item from me appears on X, it is also published on this website.

The final piece of content on the right is my favorite third-party video of the week titled *Insightful Videos*. It is published on Wednesdays at 7:30am with an anchor to this website for the content. This particular one is on Artificial Intelligence going rogue from the *Economist*.

As you read this section, you might be thinking that all this is overwhelming. But remember, this is my fifth generation of the website. As I did, you can start with a simpler version and evolve it as you assess your audience's response.

The value of this personal website has been substantial to my personal brand. Because of this website, plus all the other content that I generate on social media channels, when you Google my name, I am either on the first or second page of results.

THE SECRET TO THE NO LONGER SECRET FORMULA

o The process to building a personal brand using social media and even a website dedicated to you is evolutionary. You can and should start small and add incremental items to your brand story as you measure audience response.

o Automation is your most important asset that you need to leverage to grow your brand. Invest in the tools to tell your story, especially, if possible, research and a social media scheduling calendar.

o Clear thinking about the themes that represent your personal brand are critical to the formula for success with a maximum of three being the target.

o Consistency to the point of taking on the challenge of never missing ONE single post is important to building an audience. You can use social media calendars to make this a lot easier, including, as I originally did, scheduling an entire social media week during a Saturday or Sunday morning.

o Having thematic consistency is helpful in your social media calendar as this trains your audience to look for that content. In my case, top three of the week – brilliant research, smart infographic, and insightful video – appear at the same time every week.

o Build into your plan a personal website to consolidate your social media story and elevate your presence on Google. Use anchors to link content to your personal website.

The secret to success is having a plan, executing it aggressively, and adjusting as your audience responds. More importantly, let's not forget the opening quote from Mark Twain for this chapter, 'The secret to getting ahead is getting started.' What are you waiting for?

SUMMARY

o My initial formula was not perfect. It was probably too wide in ideas, but it formed the impetus to get started and that is the most important step.

o Create a hypothesis for your personal brand that is a combination of what you stand for and the social media channels that allow you to elevate its value. Begin experiments in those social media channels to test your ideas. Periodically check in with your audience either through engagement or surveys to adjust the journey as necessary.

o News aggregator sites are an invaluable tool to automate the research, support others that are generating important articles, inspire your own content, and differentiate your value-added messaging to the world.

o Always use a social media calendar automated tool to optimize scheduling. Test and retest your channels to assess which times generate the best engagement.

o Build into your plan a personal website to consolidate your social media story and elevate your presence on Google. Use anchors to link content to your personal website.

o Edit, enhance, improve my 'no longer secret formula' to get started.

o How you choose to create your personal brand may be different to me, based on the particular specific skills you are trying to highlight to the world.

o Critically, you need to have a formula, automate it as much as possible, and add resources to growing the value of you brand as your level of monetization increases.

REFLECTIONS

HOW WOULD YOU DESCRIBE YOUR LIFE
TODAY VERSUS 10 YEARS AGO AND HOW
COULD YOU USE A PERSONAL BRAND TO
TRANSFORM IT?

IF YOU ARE IN A CORPORATE ROLE,
HOW DO YOU THINK YOUR EMPLOYER WILL
RESPOND TO THE CREATION OF YOUR
PERSONAL BRAND?

HOW ARE YOU APPROACHING SOCIAL
MEDIA TODAY IN TERMS OF POSTING
SCHEDULE AND ARE YOU ATTRACTING THE
RESPONSE YOU EXPECTED?

HOW COULD YOU ADAPT THIS FORMULA
TO SHOWCASE YOUR SKILLS?

CHAPTER 7

STRATEGIES FOR MONETIZING YOUR PERSONAL BRAND

> 'TIMING HAS ALWAYS BEEN A KEY ELEMENT IN MY LIFE. I HAVE BEEN BLESSED TO HAVE BEEN AT THE RIGHT PLACE AT THE RIGHT TIME.'
>
> BUZZ ALDRIN,
> SECOND US ASTRONAUT TO WALK
> ON THE MOON ON JULY 20, 1969

As you continue reading this book, you may still be thinking that the success of my personal brand was down to the fact that I started it in the early days of social media. I was, indeed, lucky that LinkedIn decided to transition from a resumé site to a publishing platform and invited me to join their transformational journey. Social media, and specifically LinkedIn as my primary platform, was the impetus to finding my global audience.

The idea, however, was not served to me on silver platter. It was sparked by the belief that the world was changing and showcasing personal skills beyond your current employer would become a much more important variable to future success. In those early pioneering social media days, there was little clarity in terms of what would resonate to increase personal value. The dawn of social media was the first major opportunity to elevate the value of a personal brand.

Being first to something carries a lot of risk. As with Buzz Aldrin, coming in second provided the critical prior knowledge to de-risk and improve the experience. Your timing is actually better than mine as the possibilities to monetize your personal brand have dramatically increased since I started. As this chapter will explain, the second even larger, more valuable, opportunity to monetize a personal brand is NOW.

WHAT IS INFLUENCER MARKETING?

Welcome to the creator economy where individuals with unique differentiated brands and ready access to global audiences have emerged, according to Goldman Sachs, as one of the biggest developments of the digital age. Over the next 5 years, the total addressable market of the creator economy could roughly double in size from $250 billion today to $480 billion by 2027.[1]

As you are about to discover, your personal brand is the valuable entry ticket to the creator economy. Lots of options are available for you to mix, match and multi-dip into various revenue streams which you can customize to meet the current and future objectives of your brand.

Influencers, which are the epicenter of the creator economy have:[2]

o The power to impact purchasing decisions of others because of perceived authority, knowledge, position or relationship with their specific captive audience.

o An established distinct, defined, niche audience with whom the influencer actively engages on a regular basis.

o Social relationship assets which product brands can collaborate with to achieve defined marketing objectives.

'Influencers in social media are people who have built a reputation for their knowledge and expertise on a specific topic. They make regular posts about that topic on their preferred social media channels and generate large followings of enthusiastic, engaged people who pay close attention to their views. Brands love social media influencers because they can create trends and encourage their followers to buy products they promote.'[3]

According to McKinsey, the influencer economy will be valued at $16.4 billion in 2023.[4] Successful influencer marketing campaigns are based on authenticity. Matching relationships between brand messaging and the influencer's target audience increases engagement. Odds towards a purchase for a branded product increase as influencers who share the same core values endorse products.

Influencer marketing monetization models typically combine the following:[5]

o A flat rate per post paid to the influencer that features a product or service which is known as a brand deal. The rate can be 3 to 5 figures, even for an influencer without millions of followers or a global profile. Celebrities can charge 6 figures or more per post.

o Inclusion of links to a purchase gateway from a post published by an influencer. Every time a follower or viewer buys the product by clicking through the link or using a promo code, the influencer earns an affiliate commission.

'Influencer marketing should be about more than scoring posts endorsing your products; it should be about building real relationships with creators - you want them truly behind your brand.'[6] A well-executed influencer marketing campaign leads to greater loyalty towards the product and, more importantly, increased word-of-mouth positive advertising.

Here are some key stats to reinforce the value of individually endorsed marketing:[7]

o 88% of consumers place the highest level of trust in word-of-mouth recommendations from people they know.

- 74% of consumers identify word-of-mouth as a key influencer in their purchasing decisions.
- 28% of consumers say word-of-mouth is the most important factor in strengthening or eroding brand affinity.
- 28% of people say that word-of-mouth increases brand affinity (a customer's common values with a brand).

Customers acquired through word-of-mouth promotion spend 200% more than the average customer.

Brands that create an emotional connection receive 3 times more word-of-mouth marketing mentions than those that don't.

Influencer marketing is becoming so popular that even animals and virtual non-living AI versions are emerging. Nearly 3 million people follow a menagerie of foxes, chinchillas, opossums and reptiles on JuniperFoxx.[8] The AI enabled robot influencer Lil Miquela, created by a startup in Los Angeles, also has a following of 3 million.[9]

MEGA SOCIAL MEDIA INFLUENCERS

There are multiple levels of social media influencers in the creator economy. At the zenith are the mega influencers with 1 million followers or more on their social media channels. Typically, they are likely to be A-list celebrities and in real life and could include singers, actors or athletes.

Some of these mega influencers have an astronomical number of followers. As of January 2023, the top 10 social media mega stars across the popular platforms of Instagram, Facebook and X (formally Twitter) included:[10]

1. **CRISTIANO RONALDO** football (soccer) player – 787 million
2. **LIONEL MESSI** football (soccer) player – 530 million
3. **SELENA GOMEZ** entertainer – 499 million
4. **JUSTIN BIEBER** entertainer – 477 million

5. **KYLIE JENNER** member of Jenner / Kardashian reality TV family – 450 million

6. **KIM KARDASHIAN** member of Jenner / Kardashian reality TV family – 450 million

7. **DWAYNE 'THE ROCK' JOHNSON** actor – 435 million

8. **TAYLOR SWIFT** entertainer – 408 million

9. **KATY PERRY** entertainer – 395 million

10. **ARIANA GRANDE** entertainer – 391 million

By social media platform, let's now analyze the current leaders. As of May 2023, the top 10 most followed individuals on X were:[11]

1. **ELON MUSK** entrepreneur from Tesla, SpaceX, multiple other companies including X – 140.7 million

2. **BARACK OBAMA** former US President – 132.5 million

3. **JUSTIN BIEBER** entertainer – 112.7 million

4. **CRISTIANO RONALDO** football (soccer) player – 108.5 million

5. **RIHANNA** entertainer – 108.3 million

6. **KATY PERRY** entertainer - 107.9 million

7. **TAYLOR SWIFT** entertainer – 92.7 million

8. **NARENDRA MODI** Prime Minister of India – 88.7 million

9. **DONALD TRUMP** former US President – 86.9 million

10. **LADY GAGA** entertainer – 84.5 million

The top 10 most followed individuals on LinkedIn as of April 2023 included:[12]

1. **BILL GATES** former Microsoft CEO, Co-Chair of the Bill & Melinda Gates Foundation – 38.8 million

2. **RICHARD BRANSON** founder of the Virgin Group – 19.8 million

3. **JEFF WEINER** former LinkedIn CEO – 10.7 million

4. **ARIANNA HUFFINGTON** founder and CEO of Thrive

5. **HUFFINGTON POST** – 10.2 million

6. **SATYA NADELLA** CEO of Microsoft – 9.9 million

7. **MARK CUBAN** entrepreneur – 7.6 million

8. **TONY ROBBINS** motivational speaker – 7.2 million

9. **MELINDA FRENCH GATES** co-founder of the Bill & Melinda Gates Foundation – 7.1 million

10. **SIMON SNEAK** author and motivational speaker – 6.2 million

11. **DANIELA GOLEMAN** author psychologist and science journalist – 5.6 million

The top 10 most followed individuals on Instagram as of April 2023 were:[13]

1. **CRISTIANO RONALDO** football (soccer) player – 577 million

2. **LIONEL MESSI** football (soccer) player – 456 million

3. **SELENA GOMEZ** singer and actress – 412 million

4. **KYLIE JENNER** member of the Kardashian family and beauty products mogul – 387 million

5. **DWAYNE 'THE ROCK' JOHNSON** actor and former wrestler – 375 million

6. **ARIANA GRANDE** entertainer – 367 million

7. **KIM KARDASHIAN** TV star and businesswoman – 353 million

8. **BEYONCÉ** entertainer – 305 million

9. **KHLOE KARDASHIAN** another member of the Kardashian family – 304 million

10. **JUSTIN BIEBER** entertainer – 286 million

As of March 2023, the top 10 most followed on Facebook were:[14]

1. **CRISTIANO RONALDO** football (soccer) player – 162 million
2. **MR BEAN** British TV character played by Rowan Atkinson – 136 million
3. **SHAKIRA** entertainer – 121 million
4. **WILL SMITH** actor – 114 million
5. **LIONEL MESSI** football (soccer) player – 114 million
6. **VIN DIESEL** actor – 106 million
7. **RIHANNA** entertainer – 103 million
8. **EMINEM** entertainer – 95 million
9. **JUSTIN BIEBER** entertainer – 92 million
10. **NEYMAR DA SILVA SANTOS JUNIOR** football (soccer) player – 88 million

YouTube operates on a subscriber model where users are invited to sign up to channels that they like. As of May 2023, the top 10 YouTube global most subscribed channels were:[15]

1. **T-SERIES** an Indian record label and film production house famous for Bollywood soundtracks and pop music – 242 million
2. **COCOMELON NURSEY RHYMES** 3D animated videos of children's songs and nursery rhymes – 159 million
3. **SET** India Sony Entertainment Television (SET) India airing mix of dramas and reality shows – 156 million
4. **MR BEAST** viral stunts videos – 155 million
5. **PEWDIEPIE** Let's Play 'gaming' content – 111 million
6. **KIDS DIANA SHOW** featuring 7 year old Diana and her brother Roma and their stories – 110 million
7. **LIKE NASTYA** 8 year old Nastya Anastasia Radzinskaya telling her stories – 105 million
8. **VLAD AND NIKI** another kid series that went from opening toys on video to signing a deal with Hong Kong's Playmate Toys – 96.6 million

9. **WWE** World Wrestling Entertainment channel – 94.9 million

10. **ZEE MUSIC COMPANY** founded in Mumbai, it is a direct competitor to T-Series – 95.1 million

The top 10 influencers on TikTok as of April 2023 were:[16]

1. **KHABY LAME** wordless amusing responses to overly complicated 'life-hack' videos - 156 million

2. **CHARLI D'AMELIO** started with dance videos - 150 million

3. **BELLA POARCH** video lip-syncing - 92 million

4. **ADDISON RAE** dance videos - 88 million

5. **MR BEAST** attention grabbing 'stunts' videos first to cross over 100 million subscribers on YouTube - 80 million

6. **ZACH KING** 6 seconds magic trick videos - 75 million

7. **KIMBERLY LOIZA** make-up hair tutorials singing videos – 74 million

8. **WILL SMITH** actor – 73 million

9. **CZNBURAK** Turkish food recipes videos – 70 million

10. **DWAYNE 'THE ROCK' JOHNSON** actor – 70 million

Of course, as a mega influencer, monetizing your personal brand is much easier. A report by D'Marie Analytics, for example, estimated that a single post by Beyoncé is worth $1 million in advertising value.[17]

Some of you may find these lists of mega influencers discouraging. You might be thinking, I don't have the kind of talent of all these mega stars have. If this is how you read these lists, then you did not look carefully enough at each one.

Indeed, there are mega talented individuals that excel in entertainment and sports. There are also multiple examples that should provide you with inspiration of the possibilities on letting the world understand your unique capabilities through a public personal brand.

Review again the YouTube top 10 list. Note the success of children in building massive followings on this channel. At every age, you can showcase yourself and monetize your talents.

On the TikTok list, outside of Will Smith and Dwayne 'The Rock' Johnson, I have never heard of any of the other names present in the top 10. However, the person at the top of TikTok's list should totally inspire your journey to get started NOW. Khaby Lane is a 22 year old Senegalese born social media influencer who lives in Italy. He worked in a factory before losing his job due to the pandemic. He turned to TikTok and quickly built up a following, gaining popularity delivering wordless, amusing responses to overly complicated 'life-hack' videos. Celebrity Net Worth estimates that Khaby now has a net worth of $15 million.[18]

YOU CAN BE A MACRO, MICRO OR NANO INFLUENCER

You can and should aspire to be a mega influencer as you outline your personal plan for future financial independence. This, however, should be your aspiration and not your just near-term destination.

There are multiple other levels of social media influencers that allow you to monetize your brand. You can, in other words, make a lot of money along the way as you travel through different tiers of social media influencers.

Macro Influencers

Below mega influencers are macro influencers. This level tends to have between 100,000 to 1 million followers across social media networks.[19] This is the level I am currently in and I can confirm that I am happy with the monetary results it is delivering.

Macro influencers typically have created their own journey to fame through online specialized articles or blogs and even video blogs. Individuals in this tier spend their time becoming experts in their field and attract an audience by being recognized as thought leaders in their particular subject. They produce content regularly in multiple formats to keep their audience engaged.

My primary content includes thought leadership articles that I publish across multiple platforms including my own personal branding website. Additionally, I also share content in a dedicated YouTube channel as well as podcasts, webinars and speaking at industry conferences.

Monetization in my particular case did not start by being paid to write sponsored content. The writing was to cement industry credibility in retail, innovation and leadership topics. The monetization, which I will shortly explain, was from industry activities as options to make money from my brand.

Micro Influencers

Below macro are micro influencers of which several successful ones were mentioned in Chapter 5. This tier has followers somewhere between 1,000 and 100,000 individuals.[20]

Micro influencers are even further niched and are again considered experts in the topic selected. Typically, the smaller audience carries higher loyalty which can be exploited by brands. The US retailer 'Banana Republic handpicked a team of fashion-based micro influencers to post pictures of themselves in the brand's clothing, helping them reach previously hidden audiences'.[21]

Nano Influencers

As also indicated in Chapter 5, nano is a smaller tier, typically including fewer than 1,000 followers.[22] The social media influencers in this category have the strongest influence on their audience based on interests, community and even family ties. Examples could include council leaders, educators or health care workers.

Note there is no set rule to the tiers identified other than general definitions. Another publication defines each level as:[23]

- Nano at 1,000 to 10,000 followers
- Micro at 10,000 to 50,000
- Mid tier of macro at 50,000 to 1,000,000
- Mega at over 1,000,000

WHICH TIER SHOULD I STRIVE FOR?

When it comes to social media tiers, size does not matter. Most critical is the influence the social media influencer has on their targeted audience.

The key points to remember from all these tiers are:

1. Outside mega, which is typically based on celebrity or sports status, the rest are projections of personal expertise in building an audience. It is not the stardom from other areas, but a conscious effort through a personal brand creation process.

2. The size of the audience depends on the niche level of expertise you are projecting as a personal brand and how it resonates with the target individuals in your group.

3. The authenticity you project to your target audience and their willingness to engage with you on the thought leadership journey is what determines your value.

4. Properly executed personal branding has high value even in tiers with a fewer number of followers as the smaller audience allows you to increase your authenticity and builds greater trust.

5. Visibility of the value that your personal brand delivers at whatever level you are is critical. At every level, you must market yourself.

6. Note that Banana Republic is going to smaller groups to widen their audience. This is a trend that will only increase over time as social media is equalizing who can monetize their unique talents.

7. As social media is global, your audience does not necessarily need to be isolated to one country. You can and should strive to move through the tiers as that elevates the monetization value of your brand.

8. Achieving mega status does not require you being a celebrity or a sports star. It requires understanding your unique talents and which social media channels best optimize their visibility and monetization. Just like there is no set rule to the size of the audience in each influencer tier, there is also no set concrete definition on monetization approaches to your personal brand.

If you do decide that influencer marketing is the direction you want to take to monetize your brand, here are some general indications regarding how much money it is possible to make.[24]

o   The unspoken industry standard is $100 per 10,000 followers plus extras for type of post (x number of posts). Also, additional factors such as the industry you are in or how well you market your services all factor into your potential total rate.

o   If you engage in affiliate marketing where a business rewards affiliates for each customer brought by the affiliate's marketing efforts (you are the influencer), you can generally make 5% to 30% commission on affiliate marketing contracts.

o   On Instagram, a nano influencer can make $195 per post for a mid tier to macro, ranging from $1,221 to $1,804 per post.

o   On TikTok, nanos are at $181, macro at $531 and mega in the range of $1,631 to $4,370 per video.

o   On X, nanos can make $65 and micro can make $125 per post.

o   On Facebook, nanos are $170 and micro are at $266 per post.

Again, the above monetary values are just indicators of potential. There is no set rule that this is what they need to pay you for your social media services. It comes down to perceived value delivered and the impact the target audience makes in the influencer's marketing campaigns. Putting it more bluntly, if you make a recommendation on a specific product, does a portion of the audience you are engaging with actually buy the product?

A major side benefit of developing a personal brand is that you spend more time improving the value of the most important person in the world: YOU. As this book has already outlined, creating a personal brand requires you to clearly understand your motivations, identify your strengths and weaknesses and, more importantly, increase the visibility of your unique selling propositions (USPs). It is those USPs that increase in value as you craft and share more intensively your personal brand with your target audience.

You are already at an advantage. By reading this book you are benefiting from being introduced to the formulas that worked in my particular case. I am also exposing to you all my mistakes along the way in order to help you focus on what is more important in building a positive future based on your skills. Personal branding is a methodology to increase the value of our skills, help others improve their particular idea or solution and get paid for those services.

If you recall, I started my personal branding journey almost in spite because I did not receive the coveted major corporate promotion. The night I crafted my plan, I had no idea what target audience I would actually attract. Yet the introspection of my personal skills led to a focus on retail, emerging technology innovation and leadership. Unveiling my brand to the world required research to increase my skills in these areas so I could write about them, initially in Google blogs.

Ralph Waldo Emerson once wrote that 'life is a journey, not a destination'.[25] I can confirm, as every day I am finding improvements, 'personal branding is a journey, not a destination'.

As was the case with me, one of the greatest skills that I was able to monetize through my personal brand was consulting. Experts are needed more than ever.

Consider the following statistics on the growth of the consulting industry:[26]

- o Management consulting which deals with strategy, organization and operations, was worth $148 billion in 2020 and will grow to $243 billion by 2027.
- o IT consulting helps businesses improve the use of their technology and was worth $426 billion in 2020 with an annual growth rate of 3.5% from 2016 to 2021.
- o Human resources consulting focuses on HR topics such as recruitment, training and development and was valued $28.6 billion 2020 with growth rate of 3.1% from 2016 to 2021.

The above examples illustrate that companies will pay a lot of money for consultants. Your skills may lead you into areas you had not planned and provide alternative options for monetization.

This was the case with my personal brand. All those articles, posts, and later videos on retail, innovation and leadership attracted the startup community in Silicon Valley. I was invited to San Francisco and participated in an accelerator program where twice a year, pre-pandemic, I would listen to pitches from leading new companies from around the world.

The group hosting the event in Silicon Valley would screen over 300 companies and in each cycle have 25 of them travel to California to present their solutions. Each startup had 3 minutes to make their pitch to invitees such as myself who in turn could act as advisors or investors to selected companies post the event.

Ahead of time, the invitees would also receive a list of the 25 candidates scheduled to present. Each of us, as potential investors or advisors, could select three companies for a deeper dive into their particular solution.

These startup immersion trips to Silicon Valley were truly inspirational and I mentored a few selected companies in this process as part of an equity sharing program. The pandemic was a severe disruptor to these trips, but the lessons learned I have now transitioned to other opportunities.

I became an advisor on a monthly consulting fee basis to an artificial intelligence computer vision technology company based out of Europe. I joined and monetized multiple consulting opportunities that are prevalent on the internet which match experts with investors looking to invest in new technologies or companies.

In May 2023, I joined a group of former senior technology executives which in essence is doing the same, but with companies in post startup stages in both the US and Europe.

Equity was the compensation for the startup phase for the consulting in helping companies grow. Consulting fees followed with selected companies where I had an interest in the technology. Another group that I joined in 2023, favours a commission-based compensation structure based on new business generated from introductions to my network.

By default, a personal brand is projecting that you are an expert in something. With the proper marketing leveraging social media, you can and should monetize that something and consulting is one of the places to start.

THE BOARD OF DIRECTORS IS MEETING NOW

The expertise generated and manifested through a personal brand can also be monetized through industry or company boards. This is an area that has been highly successful for me personally as I enjoy spending time with other senior leaders in steering companies to much greater success.

There are multiple board types, of course. My focus on technology led me to two Board of Directors positions in Philadelphia on the East Coast of the United States and again in Silicon Valley on the West Coast.

Board of Directors positions are coveted because they have limited time requirements but can be highly compensated either through a quarterly stipend or through stock in the company, or both. The opportunity to be on these boards emerges from having increased presence in the industry and through a personal brand showcasing expertise that you can help that particular company grow.

Some interesting statistics about Boards of Directors positions:[27]

o The median compensation in 2021 for boards of directors was $44,850, a 5% increase from the year before.

o Not surprisingly, the most lucrative assignments go to directors of S&P 500. Average compensation for those companies was $304,856 which is a 43% increase over 10 years.

o In 2018, the top payer for a board seat was Goldman Sachs Group Inc which paid its directors an average of $599,279.

An additional approach that you can take which has been fruitful in building my personal brand is to join industry groups' Boards of Advisors. I am on multiple of these. Boards of Advisors are extremely useful as they often include decision makers which you can leverage to either help other companies grow or even monetize your own brand with them.

It is my personal brand and the value that it projects that has led companies to invite me to join their Boards of Directors and even their Boards of Advisors. Reaching this level is possible and, as it was for me, can be an apex for your transformed, more valuable career and life.

PUBLIC SPEAKING YOUR WAY TO GREATER VALUE

For some of you, the mere mention of public speaking will send you to the nearest closet to hide. Recall that I labelled myself as a closet introvert. In the beginning, I would sweat bullets just prior to getting on stage. A few times, I even had panic attacks and had to retreat to a quiet place to regain my composure.

Mark Twain once said, 'Do the thing you fear most and the death of fear is certain'.[28] You need to think of public speaking as building a muscle. The more you use or exercise that muscle, the stronger you will get. If you want to build a broader stronger personal brand, public speaking is an art you need to master or, at the minimum, be comfortable with.

Today, because of Smartphones, it is much easier to practice and improve your skills. Start by recording yourself and listening to the playback. Address flaws in how you are delivering your message. Share the videos with friends and family and ask for their advice.

If you are presenting at work, leverage key words in presentations to trigger ideas to ensure you cover the topic fully. Practice eye contact with your audience.

Public speaking is a skill all of us can learn and attain a comfort level which, if you wish, can be monetized. Generally, here is what you can expect as compensation from public speaking:[29]

- o If you are new to this and still trying to establish a brand, you can expect $500 to $2,500 per speech.
- o If your personal brand is gaining traction, the range can be $2,500 to $10,000.
- o For a well-established brand with lots of testimonials, a few books and media interviews, the range jumps to between $10,000 and $20,000.
- o For an expert in a field, you can start at $20,000 and go much higher. People with strong personal brands can charge upwards of $150,000 for a single speech.

Public speaking is another way that I have been able to monetize my brand successfully. With the increased confidence you will experience during the process of creating your own personal brand, it can and should be an option for you.

OTHER WAYS TO MONETIZE YOUR PERSONAL BRAND

While undertaking intensive research for this book, I watched numerous YouTube videos on personal branding. One of them was from Gary Vaynerchuk, a mega social media influencer who has over 30 million followers across multiple channels.[30]

In that video, Gary shared that if you follow the PP formula, you will have endless ways to monetize your brand. The first P is for *Passions* and focusing your efforts in discovering them. The second P is for *Patience* in consistently delivering content to eventually monetize your brand.[31]

In this chapter I have only scratched the surface on the possibilities to monetize your personal brand, the focus being on some of the ways I have been able to achieve this goal in building my brand.

Even in my case, as I write these words, I am evolving to new phases of monetization. For instance, I recently hired a publicist who is completing two new websites: one to monetize my personal content; the other to elevate my public speaking capabilities. Also, I am launching a new web video podcast series that will have 12 unique paying sponsors on the disruptive future retail technologies.

Other potential options for you to consider as ways of monetizing your brand include: content subscriptions, advertising and sponsorships on your website, selling products via ecommerce based on your brand, creating online courses and e-books based on your expertise, creating a club and selling memberships, sponsored articles that are funded by companies, establishing direct brand partnership with product companies, creating a paying newsletter, running paid webinars, marketing other people's products that fit your brand, getting paid to be a guest on someone else's content, or creating and selling a masterclass about your brand.

You can choose words through articles or blogs to monetize. Alternatively, if you are visual look at the explosion of TikTok,

YouTube and the growth of Instagram for videos and pictures.

Buzz Aldrin was correct in 1969 on the importance of timing as he took that second step on the moon. Monetization options for personal brands have dramatically increased since I started 10 years ago.

Unleash the passions within you and express your valuable USPs to the world. Stick with the journey as I did, embracing patience and testing of ideas to find those that could be best monetized.

Time is, indeed, money. Unleashing your personal brand is a journey, with the destination being a much more valuable brand in multiple time horizons.

SUMMARY

o Welcome to the creator economy where individuals with their own brands have emerged as one of the biggest developments of the digital age.

o The influencer economy is valued at $16.4 billion in 2023.

o Successful influencer marketing campaigns are based on authenticity.

o There are multiple levels of social media influencers that allow you to monetize your brand. You can make money on all levels as you move up the popularity scale.

o Achieving mega status does not require you being a celebrity or sports star. It requires understanding your unique talents and which social media channels best optimize their visibility and monetization.

o A personal brand by default is projecting that you are an expert in something. With the proper marketing leveraging social media, you can and should monetize that something and consulting is one of the places to start.

o An apex for your transformed more valuable career and life will be an invitation to join company boards.

o If you are going to take the time to increase your expertise by building a personal brand, spend some time honing your skills in telling your unique story to a live audience.

o There are endless ways to monetize your brand.

REFLECTIONS

WHO IS YOUR FAVORITE SOCIAL
MEDIA INFLUENCER TODAY AND WHY?

HOW MUCH IS YOUR PERSONAL
BRAND WORTH IN MONETARY VALUE?

WHAT TOP THREE WAYS
DO YOU BELIEVE YOU CAN MONETIZE
YOUR PERSONAL BRAND?

WHAT DO YOU FEAR THE MOST
AND WHAT IS STOPPING YOU
FACING THAT FEAR?

CHAPTER 8

THE ART AND SCIENCE OF SELF-PROMOTION

'WITHOUT PROMOTION,
SOMETHING TERRIBLE HAPPENS... NOTHING!'

PT BARNUM

In a 2015 personal leadership article I wrote, 'The road to success starts with a few simple steps. Be a change advocate, have an insatiable appetite for new ideas, embrace new technologies, turn your dream into goals with deadlines, and always put people first. Chase that horizon of worldwide possibilities to shape the life you always imagined and always be thankful for each milestone reached.'[1]

In that same article, I briefly mentioned the 'untold secret of great leaders' which is 'confident humility'.[2] A major benefit of building a successful personal brand is the increased confidence that you will achieve in the process. Showcasing that confidence to both your audience and potential buyers of your services requires self-promotion.

There are extremes to both confidence and humility. If you come across as too confident, your audience may end up translating this as arrogance. If humility is the major trait identified with your brand, it may be viewed as lack of confidence.

Balancing both confidence and humility is the secret to leadership and success. It is also fundamental to creating a highly differentiated personal brand that attracts investments and increases the number of options for monetization.

Human progress is typically the result of new ideas emerging, being discussed, and becoming mainstream in society. That potential is in you and using your personal brand as the megaphone to express them to the world through balanced self-promotion, leads to life changing possibilities.

In this chapter, we will explore the concept of confidence and elevate its importance by linking it to balanced humility. Additionally, we will scrutinize the art and science of self-promotion and identify best practices for leveraging promotion to increase the value of your personal brand.

TRUST IN YOUR SELF-CONFIDENCE

Dictionary.com has 2 definitions for confidence: belief in the powers, trustworthiness or reliability of a person or thing; belief in oneself and one's powers or abilities.[4] Originally from Latin and the root *fidere* meaning 'to trust', the word confidence has evolved over the centuries in its meaning. In the 1400s it meant 'assurance or belief in the good will, veracity of another'. By the mid 15th century, it had evolved to 'reliance on one's own powers, resources, or circumstances, self-assurance'. In the 1550s, we added 'certainty of a proposition or assertion with regard to a fact'.[5]

At the core of all these definitions and the historical evolution of the word confidence is trust. A successful personal brand requires an audience that trusts the leadership content and initiatives being delivered.

When trust is combined with self-confidence, the magic of a valuable brand emerges. Think back to Richard Branson and Elon Musk as examples of unstoppable personal brands that have effectively linked these two concepts in their business models.

Self-confidence without public trust typically translates to arrogance. 'While arrogance can make you feel strong and be a coping strategy for low self-esteem initially, long term arrogance is harmful. It contributes to loneliness, depression, and a lack of direction and success. It can also impact your physical health if arrogant thinking pushes you to take unnecessary risks.'[6]

Motivation to increase your self-confidence is at the core of this book. My successful branding journey placed a major focus on developing increased skills around retail, innovation and leadership which subsequently led to greater self-confidence.

As the University of South Florida points out, self-confidence is an attitude about your skills and abilities. 'It means you accept and trust yourself and have a sense of control in your life. You know your strengths and weaknesses well, and have a positive view of yourself. You set realistic expectations and goals, communicate assertively, and can handle criticism.'[7]

Self-confidence is a mental muscle we all can develop. The workout required to increase its internal and external value is on positively improving the skills you are passionate about.

According to *Psychology Today*, self-confidence is linked to almost every element involved in a happy and fulfilling life. The more confident you become, the fewer fears and anxieties will surface. Greater motivation to achieve more and more resilience to resist the effects of setbacks will become part of your psyche. Relationships will improve as ironically greater self-confidence leads to less focus on yourself.[8]

More critically, as the same publication points out, you will have a stronger sense of your authentic self. You accept who you are, including your weaknesses, knowing they are being more than mitigated by your strengths. 'Your actions will be in line with your principles, giving you a greater sense of purpose. You'll know who you are and what you stand for. You'll have the skills to show up, stand up, and speak up. In other words, you'll be able to let your best self, shine through.'[9]

As former Israeli Prime Minister Golda Meir said, 'Trust yourself. Create the kind of self that you will be happy to live with all your life. Make the most of yourself by fanning the tiny, inner sparks of possibility into flames of achievement'.[3]

EXECUTIVE PRESENCE BEGINS
AND ENDS WITH CONFIDENCE

In addition to increasing your skills in what you are projecting as your personal brand, there are other important ways of increasing your self-confidence. Here are three simple actions each of us can take:[10]

1. **SELF-AFFIRMATIONS** There is a large and growing amount of research confirming that self-affirmations reduce stress and improve confidence. Reflect back on how you succeeded in the past then verbally proclaim how that history is evidence that you will improve with the next venture. I have practiced this reminder strategy almost daily and it works.

2. **DRESS FOR SUCCESS** Research confirms that wearing formal clothes heightens feelings of confidence and authority. Additionally, when others see you dressed for success, you are viewed as more persuasive, competent and trustworthy. I leverage this extensively in my personal brand by having a dressed for success headshot across the internet and never posting anything that detracts from the image reflected in my brand.

3. **POWER MOVEMENTS** Scientific research has verified that non-verbal behaviors can alter body chemistry and enhance performance. This is a skill that I continuously try to improve. I have studied and learned different power poses which I leverage in every public representation of my brand - from photographs, to webinars, and keynotes delivered to live audiences. Again, it is a skill that can be learned.

According to economist Sylvia Ann Hewlett, there are three pillars to executive presence:[11]

o **GRAVITAS** The sum of the weight of your personality and the confidence you exude in your demeanor.

o **COMMUNICATION SKILLS** Delivered with confidence and in a concise manner.

o **PROFESSIONAL APPEARANCE** How you project yourself to others.

The common links to success always include confidence which is the pre-cursor to building trust. A self-confident individual that has taken the time to increase the value of the core skills he or she is passionate about and then concentrate these into a continuously improved personal brand will achieve exceptional results that will exceed all expectations.

SELF-CONFIDENCE COMBINED WITH HUMILITY WILL TAKE YOU TO THE NEXT LEVEL

Earlier, I introduced one of my favorite business success books called *Good to Great*. In the previous discussion, the focus was on the companies mentioned in the book and what happened to them 20 plus years later.

Good to Great also introduced the concept of Level 5 Leadership. As the author of this book, Jim Collins, summarized in the *Harvard Business Review*, 'Level 5' refers to the highest level in executive capabilities identified during their research. These leaders built enduring greatness through a paradoxical combination of personal humility plus confident professional leadership.[12]

'Level 5 leaders are a study in duality: modest and wilful, shy and fearless.'[13] *Humility traits* that they demonstrated included:[14]

o Compelling modesty, shunning public adulation, never boastful.

o Acting with quiet, calm determination and relying mainly on inspired standards, not inspiring charisma, to motivate.

o Channeling ambition into the company and not themselves. Setting up succession for continued greatness.

o Looking into the mirror to assign blame for poor results.

The *confidence leadership traits* Level 5 leaders demonstrated included:[15]

o An unwavering resolve to do whatever it takes to produce the best long-term results, no matter how difficult.

o Setting the standard in building a great company.

o Looking out the window to others to apportion credit for the success of the company.

As Level 5 leaders in *Good to Great* confirm, exceptional success is the result of balancing confidence with humility. A leader with these traits can be a major change advocate; he or she will have an insatiable appetite for new ideas, will embrace technology, focus on achievable dreams with deadlines, and will always put the people around them first. It is with these exact skills that through self-promotion you can create an exceptional, highly valuable personal brand.

THRIVE IN A DIGITALLY NOISY ADVERTISING WORLD

For a long time in my career, I fell into the trap of convincing myself that only my work should speak for my performance. There was no need to express publicly my achievements. If I worked hard and exceeded expectations, promotions and more money would follow automatically.

I can confirm from my own personal career that allowing others to define your worth based strictly on your work performance will not optimize your opportunities for both personal and professional growth. More importantly, following a strategy of letting others define you translates to less monetary rewards in the medium and longer term. The more you wait to share publicly your successes, the less net worth you will achieve.

Self-promotion is the answer to this puzzle, even if you are one of those individuals that has negative views on the concept of advertising and promotion. There is, indeed, a lot of mass media noise in our world today as these statistics confirm:[17]

o The global advertising market is worth $766 billion with 34% in USA and 18% in European Union.

o Online or digital spending makes up roughly 46% of all ad spending.

o Social media ads represent 33% of all digital spending.

o The average American now sees 4,000 to 10,000 ads per day, double what it was in 2007 and over 5 times more than in the 1970s.

Because the majority of your personal brand is today built on social media, if you embark on elevating its value as I am highly recommending, by default you need to take steps to increase visibility of your message through self-promotion. Consider these statistics on how social media is changing consumers:[18]

o Younger demographics are much more active on social media; 31% of those between the age of 16-24 find new products through paid social media ads.

o 52% of online discovery happens in public media social feeds.

o 76% of consumers have purchased a product after seeing it on a brand's social media post.

With the creation of a personal brand, you are part of the online conversation and are, by default, selling your skills and expertise as a product. Just as you cannot let others tell your story based on your work, to elevate the value of your brand, you need to engage in self-promotion.

There is a lot of good news for you in all the statistics I have just cited. You are living in the almost perfect age to create and elevate the value of a personal brand as social media is a well-established channel available to leverage. My personal brand took off when I adopted social media to showcase the value of my work. As I have already emphasised, because of the approach taken, my digital messaging grew my corporate career faster while simultaneously building a stronger personal brand.

As the second set of statistics confirm, people are leveraging social media to find new products, discover new ideas, and consummating these actions by actually buying something. If you create a durable personal brand, you are that new product, that new idea, and people will buy into it, especially if you invest in self-promotion.

BRAGGING VERSUS SELF-PROMOTION

At a personal level, the elephant in the room that stops us from engaging in self-promotion is its negative association to bragging. There is a fine line between self-promotion and bragging and crossing it may permanently damage your brand so understanding the clear distinction between the two concepts before embarking on any self-promotion strategy is crucial.

Bragging is about hyping yourself to levels that do not have facts to support them. With bragging 'we "puff" ourselves up to be greater than the quality of our work and others, and make claims with no hard data to back them up. Ultimately, bragging is creating a false narrative to make us seem bigger and better than we are and in most cases is due to insecurities.'[19]

Self-promotion works when it is based on facts. Using this strategy, you are simply elevating the visibility of your leadership activities that strengthen the value of your brand. Let me illustrate this more clearly with some examples from my social media feeds.

This 2023 LinkedIn post started with a senior executive from the USA National Retail Federation (NRF) posting about an event where we were both speaking in Silicon Valley. In that post, the NRF executive posted an image that includes my headshot picture and tagged me in his comments.

 **Tony D'Onofrio** • You
Futurist, CEO, Top 100 Retail Influencer, Board and Next-Gen Tech ...
23h • 🌐

Looking forward to joining David Johnston and the other listed great speakers at the Axis Communications Retail Leadership Forum August 14-16 in Silicon Valley with my updated edition of the "Disruptive Future of Retail" keynote presentation. JOIN US.

Thinkers360 RETHINK Retail James Stark Mike Conley, LPQ, MBA

 David Johnston • 1st
National Retail Federation | Vice President of Asset Protection & Retail...
1d • 🌐

Looking forward to being opening keynote to kick off a great forum of outstanding speakers and retail experts. Come join us at the AXIS Retail Leadership Forum August 14-16 in Sunnyvale, CA.
Tony D'Onofrio, Michele Stuart, James Stark, Mike Conley, LPQ, MBA

https://lnkd.in/eg7P_Zvz

I saw this a great opportunity to engage in self-promotion, but note the approach taken.

- o I opened by focusing on the individual that tagged me in his post with the comment that I was looking forward to joining him.

- o I added commentary on the additional speakers included in the image.

- o I then pivoted to my content, but did not brag about being part of this group or being in Silicon Valley. Instead, I highlighted the topic of my presentation and invited audiences to join us.

- o I intentionally tagged two groups that have named me a 2023 Top 100 Retail Influencer and the two hosts for the event in

California. The company hosting the event is also tagged along with the initiator of this actual post that I was re-posting.

Bragging could have been very easy in this post. Look at me, my picture, I am going to Silicon Valley, an executive of NRF mentioned my name, WOW I am special! Yet that would have been a recipe for the audience to see my brand negatively and decrease the value of this post as well as my brand.

Here is another example from LinkedIn from a keynote presentation at PGA National in Florida in 2023.

Note, I posted a picture of me as the speaker, but I did not brag about my speech or myself. Rather, I let the picture speak for itself and focused my message on thanking the organizers and recognizing their work in the excellent execution of the event. To ensure greater visibility of this post I tagged the organizers plus again the two groups that named me a top 100 global retail influencer.

By now, you should recognize some key strategies that I use in self-promotion:

1. Never brag about how great you are.

2. Focus on the individuals or groups on the other side; speaking about them elevates the value of your personal brand. Recall the *Good to Great* Level 5 leaders that always look out the window to others in delegating success.

3. Always include a picture, especially if you are in it. Research shows that people only remember 10% of what they learn after 72 hours have passed. However, if you pair a fitting image with your content, people can retain 65% of the information after 3 days.[20]

4. Include something pertinent in any engagement that relates back to you, but worded in a way that the audience will see it as a benefit to them.

5. In every self-promotion post, tag the people and the groups that are value adding your brand. In my case, I regularly include groups that place me on leadership lists.

Bragging will kill your brand and potentially your career. On the other hand, a well-executed self-promotion strategy will continuously elevate the value of your brand and lead to a greater number of opportunities.

SELF-PROMOTION AS AN EDUCATIONAL TOOL

A great strategy to leveraging self-promotion is to use it as an educational tool for your audience. This is especially valuable if coupled with how your particular social media channel is trying to differentiate their own brand.

As an example, I discovered that LinkedIn increases visibility of surveys conducted by their members and they typically receive a large number of impressions. My overall number of LinkedIn impressions as of July 19, 2023 are well over 1 million for the previous 365 days.

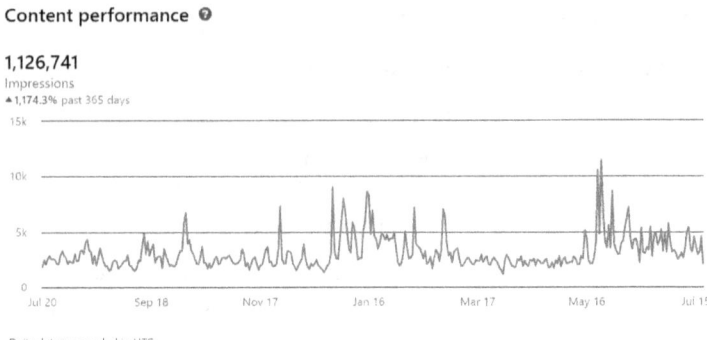

Content performance ❓

1,126,741
Impressions
▲1,174.3% past 365 days

The spikes that you see, starting in May 2023, I attribute to an intentional addition of audience surveys into my LinkedIn activities. Periodically, I ask my audience whether my posting pattern is hitting the mark for valuable content. Am I posting too little, too much, or just enough? The feedback I have received to date is that the current formula as defined in this book is exactly what the audience expects from my brand.

Lately, I have been using weekly surveys to elevate the value of my brand by linking them to events. For example, weeks before a particular keynote, I ask my LinkedIn audience for feedback on a question relevant to the presentation. I then share those results both on LinkedIn and during the actual keynote. Here is an example chart from my popular webinar on the *$9.2 Trillion Economic Impact on the Retail Industry Through 2029*[21] and in the top left you see one of those LinkedIn surveys. This particular survey asked whether Artificial Intelligence will destroy humanity, its hype and its impact will be minimal or whether it will dramatically improve our lives.

The AI Dilemma

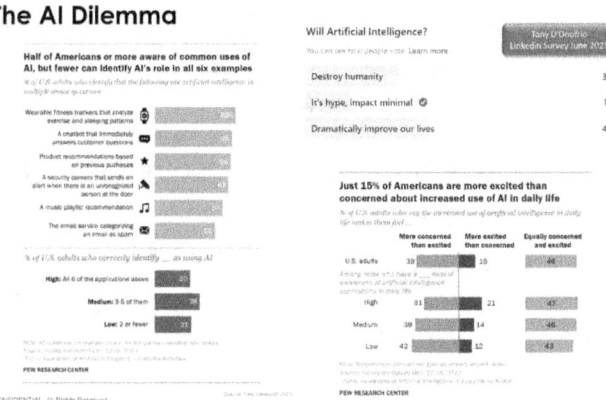

While writing this book, I have also engaged in initial self-promotion by linking surveys to its release. As an example, in this survey question, I asked the audience to vote on which social media channel is best positioned to deliver a powerful personal brand.

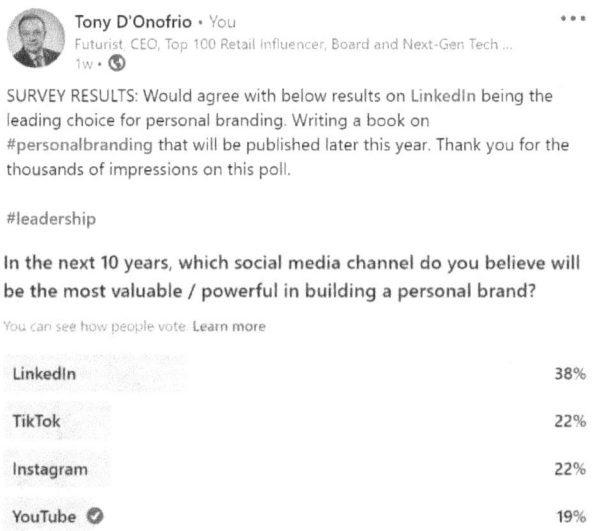

Remember that all these surveys are unscientific, but they are an optimal strategy to elevate the value of your brand by engaging your audience in conversation. This particular survey was refreshing in confirming that I personally picked LinkedIn as my primary personal branding building channel, even if I admit the results may be biased as the actual survey is on LinkedIn.

These surveys are just an example of how I engage my audience. In my personal branding formula explained in these pages, I am also leveraging the top three stories of the week - Brilliant Research, Smart Infographic, Insightful Videos - and periodic appearances of my world travel series *It's a Small World*.

The approaches you can take to showcase your brand through self-promotion are endless. Key is a unified strategy linked to your successes.

As an additional example, in May 2023, I joined a new Board of Directors in Silicon Valley. When this announcement came out, I engaged immediately in subtle self-promotion.

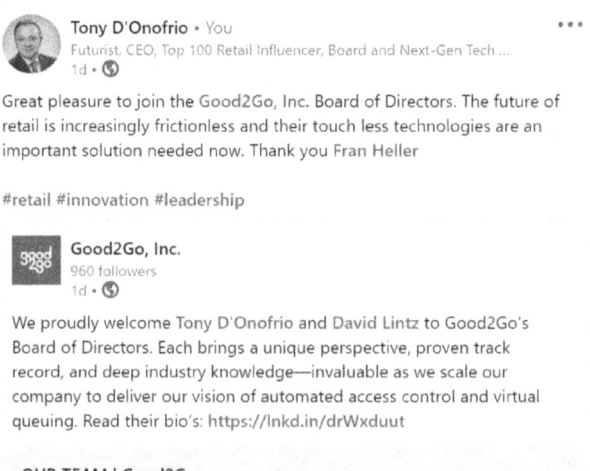

Again, in my reply, the majority of the focus was about the importance of the solutions in moving the retail industry forward through innovation. I did not mention, or even consider writing about, my unique skills or why I am great for this new Board of Director position.

Remember that the process of delivering content and engaging in self-promotion is always evolutionary. I adopted surveys into my strategy because I recognized that LinkedIn placed greater value on this feature. This may not last forever. Whatever is your preferred channel for personal branding, you need to monitor what they emphasize and integrate that strategy into your self-promotion strategy.

THE SCIENCE BEHIND SELF-PROMOTION

Promoting yourself has pitfalls that you need to avoid. If you overdo it, it can come across as arrogance; too little self-promotion leads to a weaker personal brand.

Here are a few additional research studies on the effectiveness of self-promotion in personal branding:

o Research published in *Self and Identify Journal* found that self-promotion coupled with information that substantiates the claim is associated with more favorable interpersonal evaluations compared to when the claim is unsubstantiated. Modest claims are evaluated even more than self-promotional claims.[22]

o The importance of choosing your words carefully is illustrated by a study led by Ovul Sezer of the University of North Carolina. 'Participants rated people who made comments on social media such as "Huh. I seem to have written one of Amazon.com's top 10 books of the year (so far). Unexpected" as not only less likable but also less competent than people who were more straightforward ("I have written one of Amazon.com's top 10 books of the year").'[23]

o Taking humility to extremes hurts your brand. Research conducted by Kate Barasz of ESADE and Michael Norton of the Harvard Business School found that if you are 'given an opportunity to brag—for example, by being asked, "What are your greatest strengths?" or "How did you finish that so quickly?"—foregoing it can raise suspicion. We found that not answering or being coy about such questions may cause people to think you're neither trustworthy nor likable.'[24]

o Intentionally setting up a conversation for someone to allow you to brag is worse. 'New research led by Ryan Hauser of Harvard Business School indicates that posing a question not because you want an answer but because you want someone to ask the same of you makes a worse impression than outright bragging. Let questions arise organically, and when you see opportunities to highlight your successes, make the most of them.'[25]

o It always comes down to balance. Research found that people who act narcissistic and overly positive about themselves tend to make great first impressions. 'Even seemingly excessive self-promoters tend to come off positively at first. Other people like them and rate them as agreeable, competent, and well-adjusted. But the same things that can make a person seem great at first can also end up making them look like a jerk. The initial positive impression will turn sour if the same level of self-promotion continues over time and across repeated social interactions.'[26]

o Body language is also important to self-promotion. 'Studies have found that adopting one posture will probably cause a person you're interacting with to adopt the other. This can put you right into the role of your choosing, whether you want to come across as a good leader or a follower. More recent research has shown that your posture can also dictate the content discussed an interaction. The person in the more "dominant" role will probably do most of the talking and make most of the decisions. Meanwhile, the person in the more "submissive" role isn't really expected to contribute.'[27]

Research on self-promotion gives us many clues on leveraging its effectiveness. When in doubt, the Roman statesman and scholar Marcus Tullius Cicero provided the best advice when he said, 'never go to excess, but let moderation be your guide'.[28]

PERSONAL BRANDING SELF-PROMOTION BEST PRACTICES

Self-promotion is an important ingredient to creating a powerful personal brand. Here are my favorite dozen best practices for its execution:

1. **BE YOURSELF** If you project who you really are with factual data and avoid exaggerations, your brand will be recognized as authentic. The more you stray into the imaginary bragging world, the faster you will kill your personal brand.

2. **STAY FOCUSED** Recall your unique selling propositions that you are projecting with your personal brand and stick with them.

3. **PROJECT EXPERTISE** Self-promotion works if your brand is perceived as an expert in a particular field.

4. **USE EACH SOCIAL MEDIA CHANNEL STRATEGICALLY** Not all channels are created equal when it comes to the self-promotion message you are trying to deliver. The content should dictate the social media channel selection that optimizes visibility.

5. **LEVERAGE OTHERS** Self-promotion works best when it builds on what others are saying about you.

6. **REMEMBER CONFIDENT HUMILITY** Never boast; be gracious and humble with subtle confidence expressing messaging.

7. **CONSISTENCY WINS THE DAY** Create a style that matches your personality for self-promotion and stick with it.

8. **RESPOND ON A TIMELY BASIS** Have you noticed in social media, posts tend to disappear rather quickly and we are on to the next topic? When an opportunity arises for self-promotion, act on it in a timely manner.

9. **COLLABORATE** Your brand should be built on collaborating with others. When they acknowledge your contributions, use these opportunities for self-promotion.

10. **SEEK ADVICE** If you are uncertain, ask others you trust for feedback on your self-promotion activities.

11. **MONITOR THE FEEDBACK** Make sure you review how your audience is responding to your self-promotion and make adjustments if you see issues.

12. **LOOK OUT THE WINDOW** In engaging with self-promotion, do NOT make it all about you. Praising or recognizing others is the most important part of any self-promotion strategy.

I opened this chapter with a quote from Phineas Taylor Barnum, an American showman who went on to create what he called the 'greatest show on earth', the Ringling Bros and Barnum & Bailey Circus.[29] Personal branding success requires measured, balanced and careful self-promotion for, as PT Barnum reminds us, promotion is a MAJOR critical component to greater wealth and success.

SUMMARY

o There are extremes to both confidence and humility. If you come across as too confident, your audience may end up translating this as arrogance. If humility is the major trait identified with your brand, it may be attributed to lack of confidence.

o When trust is combined with self-confidence, the magic of a valuable brand emerges. Self-confidence is a mental muscle we all can develop.

o A Level 5 leader can be a major change advocate. He or she will have an insatiable appetite for new ideas, will embrace technology, focus on achievable dreams with deadlines, and will always put the people around them first. It is with these exact skills that, through self-promotion, you can create an exceptional, highly valuable personal brand.

o Allowing others to define your worth based strictly on your work performance will not optimize your opportunities for both personal and professional growth.

o With the creation of a personal brand, you are part of the online conversation and are, by default, selling your skills and expertise as a product.

o There is a fine line between self-promotion and bragging and crossing it may permanently damage your brand.

o Whatever are your preferred channels for personal branding, you need to monitor what they emphasize and integrate that strategy into your content delivery.

o When it comes to self-promotion, the Roman statesman and scholar Marcus Tullius Cicero summarized it best when he said, 'Never go to excess, but let moderation be your guide'.

REFLECTIONS

HOW WOULD YOU DESCRIBE
YOUR LEVEL OF CONFIDENCE
IN YOURSELF TODAY?

WHAT IS YOUR FAVORITE BUSINESS
BOOK AND WHAT LESSONS DID IT
CONTAIN THAT YOU CAN LEVERAGE
INTO A PERSONAL BRAND?

HAVE YOU EVER BRAGGED ABOUT
SOMETHING AND CAN YOU
RECALL THE REACTION?

HOW DILIGENT ARE YOU IN
RECOGNIZING OTHERS IN A TEAM
SETTING VERSUS DOING THE
MAJORITY OF THE TALKING?

CHAPTER 9

POWER YOUR PERSONAL BRAND WITH ARTIFICIAL INTELLIGENCE

> 'ARTIFICIAL INTELLIGENCE WOULD BE THE ULTIMATE VERSION OF GOOGLE. THE ULTIMATE SEARCH ENGINE THAT WOULD UNDERSTAND EVERYTHING ON THE WEB.
>
> LARRY PAGE

In today's world, your personal brand is built on everything you either publish or others say about you on the internet which is summarized and analyzed by search engines such as Google. As the second part of Page's quote reminds us, we are not that far away from a world where Artificial Intelligence (AI) analyzes deeper and faster the vast amounts of information published on the internet with AI defining your online persona, whether you are active or inactive in defining it, in mere seconds.

On the positive side, AI will dramatically improve the productivity you can achieve in creating a stronger, faster, more valuable personal brand. What used to take hours or days to research and crystalize your content, now takes seconds. From blogs, to images, videos and podcasts, the quality of your content can potentially be increased with the use of Artificial Intelligence.

Beware that on the risk side, this means any negative published news about you will also travel faster. As a result, AI will elevate the importance of checking everything you publish online regularly, especially any profile information.

In this chapter, we will explore the trends that are accelerating technology adoption and how digital transformation can be applied to personal brands. We look at how AI can be actioned in the delivery of your brand and the tools available to facilitate this process. Finally, we conclude with some fascinating examples of how AI is disrupting the future of personal branding.

DIGITAL TRANSFORMATION IS CRITICAL TO YOUR BRAND

There are numerous examples across industries that explain the evolution of technology and how it is changing the world faster. The hottest buzzwords in all industries today that capture how technology is being adopted are 'digital transformation'.

As I wrote in a 2023 article, linking digital with transformation was an evolutionary process that started in the 1970s when computer-aided designs and manufacturing were first used in business. The 1980s saw the addition of enterprise resource planning, followed by customer relationship management in the 1990s.[1]

The objective of these computer solutions was to improve efficiency and productivity by digitizing manual processes. 'In the late 1990s, we saw the rise of eCommerce and online banking. These activities were initially carried out offline but were later moved online as internet speeds increased. This was followed by the introduction of social media in the mid 2000s, which revolutionized how we communicate and share information.'[2]

The pace of change is accelerating. Survival as a company today requires intensive focus on increased digital connectivity with consumers and markets.

Here are some interesting statistics about our increased digitized world:[3]

o 70% of organizations either have a digital transformation strategy or are currently working on one.

o Global spending on digital transformation is expected to reach $6.8 trillion by 2023.

o 87% of business leaders think that digital transformation will disrupt their industries.

o Digitally mature companies are 23% more profitable than their less mature peers.

o The success rate of digital transformation is below 30%.

So, what does this have to do with your personal brand, you might ask? The fact is, digital transformation is disrupting individuals and not just industries. Your personal brand is the Me.Inc company and, as an enterprise that wants to monetize value, all these statistics apply to you as individual.

With the increased adoption of digital channels, today you have a greater opportunity to showcase your intrinsic value to your audience. Monetization follows when you can demonstrate a positive Return-on-Investment (ROI).

Not that you need to achieve 100% success with every personal branding activity. As the above data confirms, the success rate for industries with digital transformation is below 30%.[4] You will make mistakes. Get comfortable with these, learn from them and pivot quickly to improvements to keep your target audience engaged. Artificial intelligence, as you are about to discover, will make successful digital transformation easier.

In my *Disruptive Future of Retail* keynote presentation that I have delivered thousands of times around the world, there are two mainstay charts that receive minimal updates. Here is the first:[5]

Technology Global Power Shifts Accelerating

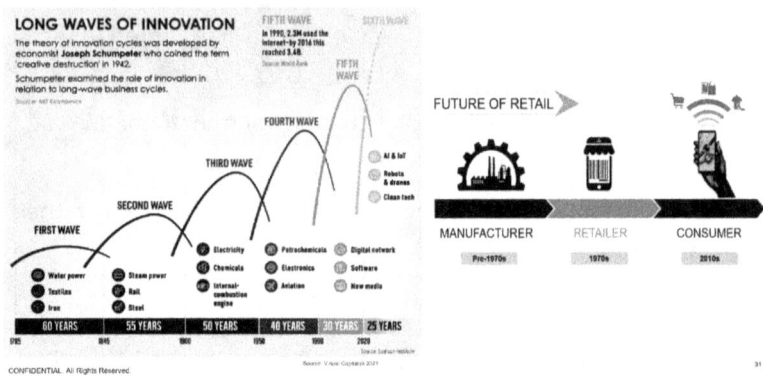

As the *Long Waves of Innovation* section of this chart illustrates, technology disruption is not new. From the Industrial Revolution forward, new waves of technology disruptions have emerged.[6]

The theory of innovation cycles was developed by economist Joseph Schumpeter, who coined the term 'creative destruction' in 1942. This theory suggests that business cycles operate under long waves of innovation with markets often disrupted and key clusters of industries having outsized effects on the economy.[7] The introduction of the railroad, for example, at the turn of the 19th century reshaped urban demographics and trade. Similarly, the internet disrupted entire industries – from retail to media.[8]

Note from the chart that each successive long innovation wave is getting shorter. We are currently in Wave 6 which includes Artificial Intelligence (AI), Internet-of-Things (IoT), robots and drones and clean technologies.[9]

Post World War II, it is my belief that retail as an industry, in the long waves of innovation ecosystem, has transitioned through three major megatrends. This is depicted by the graphic on the right.

Prior to the 1970s, efficient production lines placed the power of retail primarily in the hands of manufacturers of consumer goods. In the 1970s, the power shifted to retailers with the introduction of the barcode on all consumer products. By the 2010s, with the fast adoption of the Apple iPhone, the power had transitioned to the consumer who, with a mini computer in their hands, can instantly decide where to shop from wherever they are standing. Imagine the irony of standing in a store using that brand's Wi-Fi, deciding you are not happy with the shopping experience, and instantly buying from a competitor using a smartphone.[10]

As you craft your personal brand you need to recognize that you are living in an age of accelerated digital transformation. Understanding how the world is changing around you allows you to be selective on which technologies to adopt based on your specific strengths and weaknesses and where you want to place focus. Always remember that everything around you that is digital is an opportunity to leverage and to elevate the value of your brand.

TWO FORCES ACCELERATING INNOVATION

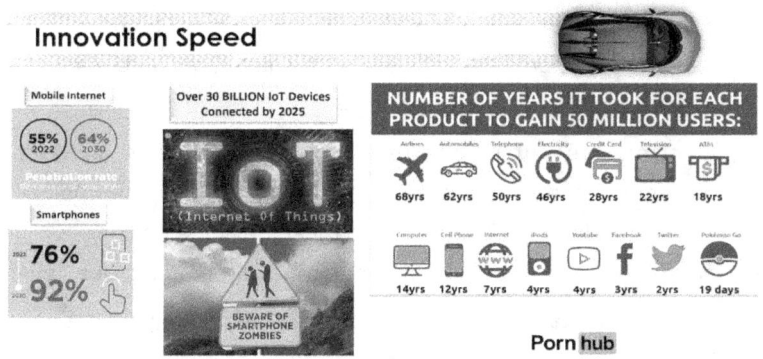

The second chart that is a mainstay in my global keynote focuses on the two forces accelerating innovation.

The first force is the mobile internet. The global internet and smarter mobile devices are connecting the majority of the world's population. Through mobile devices, by 2030, 64% of the global population will have access to the internet. A major opportunity for brands and retailers is that 92% of those connections will be on Smartphones.[11] The second major force accelerating innovation is the Internet-of-Things or the connection of billions of devices.[12]

On the right of this same key forces chart are specific technologies and how long it took to reach 50 million users. As you can see, it took the telephone 68 years, the credit card 28 years, cell phone 12 years, internet 7 years, and Pokémon Go a mere 19 days.[13] As with the long innovation waves, each new technology adoption cycle is getting shorter.

The mobile internet needs to be your most favored friend as you plan your personal brand strategy. Leveraging social media through the mobile internet is how you reach your global audience. Connected devices, especially as they are infused with AI, will be additional opportunities to explore in the future for your brand.

There are three key critical reminders that stand out from this second chart:

1. The audience at your disposal to grow a personal brand is massive and increasing as more of the global population joins the mobile internet.

2. Smartphones, with their increased digital capabilities, allow for greater connectivity and personalization of personal branding messages. Increased adoption of these devices provides access to growing a larger number of followers at a global level.

3. Time to get started is NOW. The pace of technology innovation is not stopping. In fact, it is accelerating and failure to create a personal brand leaves you behind in potentially reaching your full monetizable value.

Do you want further proof on the need to start now? ChatGPT, which was released in November 2022, reached 1 million active users in 5 days and 100 million users in just 2 months.[14] In July 2023 Meta released Threads to compete with Twitter and in one hour reached 1 million users which escalated to 100 million users in 5 days.[15]

Threads, incidentally, is a social media channel to consider for your personal branding activities. At the time of writing, it is not embedded in my personal formula as I still favor X. ChatGPT as you will soon discover, will play a larger role in the evolution of my personal brand.

PERSONAL BRANDING MEETS ARTIFICIAL INTELLIGENCE

The future of personal branding using artificial intelligence (AI) holds significant potential. Here are a few key aspects to consider:

o **AI-POWERED CONTENT CREATION** AI can assist individuals in creating personalized and engaging content for their personal brand. Natural Language Processing (NLP) models can generate blog posts, social media captions and even video scripts based on user preferences and target audience analysis.

o **INTELLIGENT SOCIAL MEDIA MANAGEMENT** AI tools can help individuals manage their social media presence more effectively. These tools can analyze audience behavior, suggest optimal posting times, recommend content ideas and even automate certain tasks like scheduling posts or responding to messages.

o **PERSONALIZED RECOMMENDATION** AI algorithms can analyze user data and provide personalized recommendations for content, products, or services that align with an individual's personal brand. This can enhance engagement and help build a loyal following.

o **CHATBOTS AND VIRTUAL ASSISTANTS** AI-powered chatbots and virtual assistants can handle routine inquiries, provide information and engage with followers on behalf of a personal brand. These AI assistants can save time and improve customer service by offering quick and accurate responses.

o **DATA ANALYTICS AND INSIGHTS** AI can analyze vast amounts of data to provide valuable insights into audience preferences, trends and performance metrics. This information can help individuals refine their personal brand strategy and make data driven decisions.

o **ENHANCED PERSONALIZATION** AI can enable personal brands to deliver highly personalized experiences to their audience. By leveraging user data, AI algorithms can tailor content, recommendations and interactions to individual preferences, increasing engagement and brand loyalty.

o **VOICE AND IMAGE RECOGNITION** AI-powered voice and image recognition technologies can enhance personal branding by enabling individuals to create unique audio or visual content. Voice assistants, podcasts and video content can help establish a distinct personal brand identity.

o **PERSONALIZED CUSTOMER EXPERIENCE** AI can enable personal brands to deliver highly personalized customer experiences. By leveraging AI-powered chatbots, recommendation engines and customer data analysis, personal brands can tailor their interactions, offers and services to individual customers, fostering stronger connections and loyalty.

o **VIRTUAL REALITY (VR) AND AUGMENTED REALITY (AR)** VR and AR technologies can enhance personal branding experiences by creating immersive and interactive content. Personal brands can use AI to develop virtual experiences, product demonstrations or virtual showrooms, allowing audiences to engage with the brand in unique and memorable ways.

o **ENHANCED TARGET AUDIENCE INSIGHTS** AI can provide deeper insights into target audiences by analyzing vast amounts of data from various sources. By understanding audience preferences, behaviors and demographics, personal brands can refine their messaging, content strategy and marketing efforts to better resonate with their target audience.

o **PERSONALIZED ADVERTISING AND MARKETING CAMPAIGNS** AI-powered advertising platforms can optimize ad targeting and delivery based on individual user preferences and behaviors. This enables personal brands to create highly targeted and personalized advertising campaigns that yield better results and higher conversion rates.

o **INFLUENCER MARKETING OPTIMIZATION** AI can play a significant role in influencer marketing by identifying the most suitable influencers for a personal brand. AI algorithms can analyze influencers' content, engagement rates and audience demographics to find the best matches for collaborations, maximizing the impact of influencer marketing campaigns.

o **SENTIMENT ANALYSIS AND REPUTATION MANAGEMENT** AI-powered sentiment analysis tools can monitor online conversations and social media mentions related to a personal brand. This helps individuals understand public sentiment, identify potential issues and proactively manage their online reputation.

o **CONTINUOUS LEARNING AND IMPROVEMENT** AI algorithms can continuously learn and adapt based on user interactions and feedback. This allows personal brands to refine their strategies, content and messaging over time, ensuring they stay relevant and engaging to their audience.

It's important to note that while AI offers numerous opportunities, personal branding still requires human creativity, authenticity and strategic thinking. AI should be seen as a tool to enhance and streamline personal branding efforts, allowing individuals to focus on building meaningful connections and delivering value to their audience.

AI CONTENT CURATED TOOLS FOR PERSONAL BRANDING

Here are a few AI-powered content creation and curation tools that could be useful for personal branding:

o **WORDSMITH** This is an AI-powered natural language generation tool that can automatically generate written content such as blog posts, social media updates and product descriptions. It uses machine learning algorithms to analyze data and create content that is tailored to the interests and preferences of specific audiences.

o **CURATA** This is an AI-powered content curation tool that can help personal brands find and share high quality content on social media and other platforms. It uses machine learning algorithms to analyze content and recommend articles and other pieces of content that are relevant to a specific audience.

o **CANVA** This is an AI-powered design tool that can help personal brands create high quality graphics and visual content. It uses machine learning algorithms to suggest design elements and layouts based on the user's preferences and the type of content they are creating.

o **ARTICOOLO** This is an AI-powered content creation tool that can automatically generate articles based on a set of keywords or topics. It uses natural language processing and machine learning to analyze data and create content that is informative and engaging.

o **LUMEN5** This is an AI-powered video creation tool that can help personal brands create engaging video content using existing written content such as blog posts or social media updates. It uses machine learning algorithms to automatically select and edit video clips and images that are relevant to the content being used.

o **HOOTSUITE INSIGHTS** This is an AI-powered social media monitoring tool that can help personal brands track and analyze social media activity. It uses machine learning algorithms to analyze data from social media platforms and identify trends, sentiment and other insights that can inform brand strategy.

o **NEWSCRED** This is an AI-powered content marketing platform that can help personal brands create, distribute and measure the impact of their content. It uses machine learning algorithms to analyze data and recommend content that is relevant to a specific audience, as well as to optimize content for maximum engagement and conversion.

o **GRAMMARLY** This is an AI-powered writing assistant that can help personal brands improve the quality of their written content. It uses natural language processing to analyze grammar, spelling and style, and provides suggestions for improvement.

o **ADOBE SENSEI** This is an AI-powered platform that can help personal brands create and manage visual content. It uses machine learning algorithms to analyze data and suggest design elements and layouts that are tailored to the specific needs and preferences of individual users.

o **IBM WATSON** This is a suite of AI-powered tools and services that can be used for a variety of purposes, including content creation, curation and analysis. It includes natural language processing, image and video recognition, and other capabilities that can help personal brands create and distribute high quality content that resonates with their audience.

o **FEEDLY** This is an AI-powered content curation tool that can help personal brands discover and share high quality content on social media and other platforms. It uses machine learning algorithms to analyze content and recommend articles and other pieces of content that are relevant to a specific audience.

- ○ **ACROLINX** This is an AI-powered content governance tool that can help personal brands ensure consistency and quality across all their written content. It uses natural language processing to analyze content and provide suggestions for improvement, as well as to ensure that content adheres to brand guidelines and style.

- ○ **COSCHEDULE HEADLINE ANALYZER** This is an AI-powered tool that can help personal brands create compelling headlines for their content. It uses machine learning algorithms to analyze word choice, structure and length, and provides a score and suggestions for improvement.

- ○ **HUBSPOT CONTENT STRATEGY TOOL** This is an AI-powered tool that can help personal brands develop a comprehensive content strategy. It uses machine learning algorithms to analyze data from social media and other sources, and recommends topics and formats that are likely to resonate with a specific audience.

- ○ **PHRASEE** This is an AI-powered tool that can help personal brands create engaging email subject lines that are likely to generate high open rates. It uses natural language processing and machine learning to analyze data and generate subject lines that are engaging and effective.

These are just a few of the many AI-powered content creation and curation tools available for personal branding. As AI technology continues to advance, we can expect to see even more sophisticated tools and services that can help personal brands create and distribute high quality content that resonates with their audience. It's important to evaluate the features and capabilities of each tool to determine which one is best suited for your specific needs and goals.

AI FOR PERSONAL BRANDING IS JUST GETTING STARTED

Did you notice anything different in the last sections you just read on *Personal Branding Meets Artificial Intelligence* and the

AI Content Curated Tools for Personal Branding? Did any words, sentences, or para-graphs seem to be misaligned in terms of the writing style compared with the rest of this book?

There is, in fact, a dramatic difference. And here's why. Both *Personal Branding Meets Artificial Intelligence* and *AI Content Curated Tools for Personal Branding* were written by ChatGPT and other online Artificial Intelligence (AI) Chatbots and have been replicated in this chapter as a small sample on the future potential for artificial intelligence.

The questions that I asked the AI online chat tools to generate this content were:

o What is the future of personal branding using artificial intelligence?

o Can you recommend any specific AI-powered content creation or curation tools for personal branding?

Every single word that you read, in just these two sections of this chapter, from the introduction to the conclusion was written by AI tools such as ChatGPT. The key benefit in leveraging these AI tools is productivity. The 1400+ words in these two sections were written by Artificial Intelligence in minutes versus hours of research if I had wanted, for example, to find all the AI curated tools available today.

Countless numbers of AI chatbot websites are now available, many free of charge, to ask your own questions using artificial intelligence. For the previous two sections I used poe.com which provides over a dozen different AI query tools.[16]

But let me give you some words of caution as you contemplate using AI to enhance your personal branding or any other online activities:

These AI tools are good at crunching lots of content and then re-arranging it quickly to answer your questions. But the process is not perfect. Multiple items listed as examples of how AI will improve the future of personal branding were repeated when I asked for more information. You are seeing the cleaned-up version where the duplicated material was deleted.

The output from AI was useful, but it lacks character in terms of representing how I want to express my personal brand. Throughout this book, with every section, I add a personal story or creative idea from the years of experience in building a personal brand. AI is a cold output of facts with no warm heart to bring it alive for the reader. As I have explained, AI tends to repeats things, even in the same query, and totally relying on its output is highly risky.

AI tools are still ingesting the vast amount of content available and they are behind a few years. As of August 2023, in poe.com, the content has ingested information through September 2021 and is therefore almost 2 years behind.[17]

If you are planning to quote any content back to original sources, you need to ask for sources as part of the queries. I did this previously in another project and multiple links generated by the AI tools did not work or were invalid. Again, this highlights that AI is not yet perfect.

Accuracy can be a challenge, too, in what AI thinks is the truth. I will explore this further in the next section.

The caution at the end of the *Personal Branding Meets Artificial Intelligence* section which was generated by AI is valid. As the chatbot stated, while AI offers numerous opportunities, personal branding still requires human creativity, authenticity and strategic thinking. AI should be seen as a tool to enhance and streamline personal branding efforts, allowing individuals to focus on building meaningful connections and delivering value to their audience.

AI can give you data faster to tell your story, but it is how your audience perceives you as an individual, your personality, that will make you valuable to a targeted audience.

There is no doubt, AI will revolutionize research and speed up the ability to generate fresh content. But just using AI as your content is a dangerous strategy as it will come across as robotic.

Someday, AI may reach true artificial consciousness. Until then, think of AI as a tool to improve what made you successful in the first place, success that you now want to transition to a powerful personal brand.

AI ACCELERATES PERSONAL BRANDING CREATIVITY

Digital acceleration of new AI technologies is ushering other challenges that could impact personal brands. Deep fakes are one of them, especially if your personal brand becomes popular.

According to a 2023 essay published in the *Wall Street Journal*, 'Because of advances in computing power, smarter machine learning algorithms and larger data sets, we will soon share digital space with a sinister array of AI-generated news articles and podcasts, deepfake images and videos - all produced at a once unthinkable scale and speed. As of 2018, according to one study, fewer than 10,000 deepfakes had been detected online. Today the number of deepfakes online is almost certainly in the millions.'[18] Deep fakes are not a near term problem in terms of personal branding for most of us, but they are a challenge we need to understand and track for potential future impact.

Another example of what the digital future has in store for us is the website character.ai.[19] This website creates an artificial intelligence experience that mimics conversations with your favorite characters, be they fictional, historical or completely new to the world. Example characters available on this website include Elon Musk, Napoleon Bonaparte, Albert Einstein, Queen Elizabeth II, William Shakespeare, Bill Gates and many more. The responses you get from each are based on what has been published and crunched by AI through the website. It is not a 'real' conversation with each of them. What does this say about how you will engage an audience in the future with a personal brand?

As I complete this book, there is a major Hollywood talent labor dispute taking place. Artificial intelligence is also at the center of this dispute as actors want strong protection against their likeness being used to train AI and potentially replace them.[20] If this an area of concern, research what you are trying to protect and, when in doubt, seek professional advice.

As an example, if you are trying to protect images, approaches you can take to safeguard yourself include opting out of AI database training sets, copywriting your work and blocking web crawlers with robots. txt. Robots.txt is a text file that can be placed in the backend code of a website to tell web crawlers what they can and cannot scan. You can use it to stop a crawler from looking at certain pages or files, which is helpful if you don't want your images to be used by AI.[21]

Artificial Intelligence is also growing a brand new category of personal branding called the virtual influencer. Lil Miquela, Imma and supermodel Shudu have collected millions of dollars from deals with fashion giants such as Dior, Calvin Klein, Chanel and Prada. These three have one thing in common, none of them are real.[22] The virtual influencer market is worth $4.5 billion and is projected to grow 26% by 2025.[23] These AI generated influencers can generate as much as $10,000 for a social media post by collaborating with major brands.[24]

As I wrote in a 2023 personal article, there is potential major risk to the full adoption of AI for humanity. In March 2023, a group of prominent scientists and tech industry leaders such as Elon Musk and Apple co-founder Steve Wozniak signed a public letter calling, 'on all AI labs to immediately pause for at least 6 months the training of AI systems more powerful than GPT-4. This pause should be public and verifiable, and include all key actors. If such a pause cannot be enacted quickly, governments should step in and institute a moratorium.'[25]

In June 2023, the EU European Parliament passed a draft law known as the AI Act which puts new restrictions on the riskiest uses of the technology. 'It would severely curtail uses of facial recognition software, while requiring makers of AI systems like the ChatGPT chatbot to disclose more about the data used to create their programs.' This initial vote is a step closer to a final version that is expected by the end of 2023. [26]

A Pew Research study published in 2023 states, 'More broadly, the public remains cautious about the impact artificial intelligence is having on American life. Just 15% say they are more excited than concerned about the increasing use of AI in daily life, compared with 38% who are more concerned than excited; 46% express an equal mix of concern and excitement.'[27]

In this section, I specifically shared how AI is already disrupting personal branding. Deep fakes, fake conversations with famous people, labor disputes and virtual influencers should be a reminder that alternatives are being sought in the fast-growing world of personal branding. There is risk in AI that we all need to be aware of, but it is already becoming ubiquitous to our lives.

ELEVATE YOUR PERSONAL BRAND
WITH ARTIFICIAL INTELLIGENCE

AI and its aggressive growth should be a wakeup call for you that it is time to step up your game and work on continuously value adding your skills. According to Accenture research, published by the World Economic Forum, 40% of all working hours could be impacted by large language models such as ChatGPT.[28]

Most at risk from AI are clerical roles which are declining quickly. On the other side of the spectrum, AI will generate higher demand for AI and machine learning specialists, data analysts and scientists and digital transformation specialists.[29]

Depending on your current work role, your job may end up being put at AI risk. This increases the urgency to create and nurture the growth of a personal brand. AI today is another tool that, as this chapter has explained, will help you achieve success faster.

To succinctly illustrate this, in poe.com, I asked ChatGPT, 'What can you tell me about the online personal brand of Tony D'Onofrio?' Here is the AI generated response describing my personal brand:[30]

Tony D'Onofrio is a recognized global business leader with over 40 years of experience in retail, security and technology. He is also a prolific writer, keynote speaker and influencer on social media platforms such as LinkedIn and X.

D'Onofrio has built a strong online personal brand by consistently sharing his insights, opinions and perspectives on various topics related to the retail industry, technology and innovation. His posts on LinkedIn and X often feature valuable industry data, analysis and predictions.

D'Onofrio's LinkedIn profile is particularly impressive, with over 550,000 followers (incorrect number). He regularly posts articles, videos and updates about his speaking engagements and other professional activities. He also engages with his followers by responding to comments and questions, which helps to build a sense of community and trust.

D'Onofrio is also a sought-after keynote speaker at industry events and conferences. He uses his speaking engagements to share his ideas and expertise on topics such as retail innovation, digital transformation and the future of retail. His speaking style is engaging, informative, and often includes real-world examples and case studies.

In addition to his online presence, Tony D'Onofrio has also been recognized for his contributions to the retail industry through various awards and honors. He was named one of the Top 100 Retail Influencers by RETHINK Retail, and he has been a recipient of the prestigious Retail Touchpoints Customer Engagement Award (Touchpoint award incorrect).

Beyond his work in the retail industry, D'Onofrio is also a passionate advocate for education and mentorship. He has served as a mentor for several industry associations and organizations, and he has been a guest lecturer at various universities and schools.

Overall, Tony D'Onofrio's online personal brand is a testament to his expertise, thought leadership and ability to engage with his audience. His strong presence on social media, combined with his speaking engagements and writing, have helped to establish him as a leading authority in the retail and technology industries. Through his thought leadership, speaking engagements, writing and involvement in industry organizations, he has become a respected and influential voice in the retail community.

There are a few inaccuracies in this summary which reflect again on the challenges of just using AI to generate content. However, if someone is searching my personal brand online, they will clearly and quickly understand both the value and direction of my work. AI delivers this content in seconds.

This AI generated analysis confirms that all my consistent efforts to grow my personal brand are working. For you, the reader, this is good news as you now have the formula framework to unleash your own valuable brand and, leveraging AI tools, reach success much faster.

The opening quote of this chapter reminds us that Google is the legacy engine that elevates the value of personal brand. As technology adoption accelerates, artificial intelligence will be the ultimate search engine to dramatically summarize in a shorter amount of time your valuable persona to potential monetizable audiences.

SUMMARY

o The increased adoption of artificial intelligence (AI) will disrupt all industries and will be a game changer for personal branding.

o Implementing AI in a branding strategy carries both risks and opportunities, especially in the near term.

o Digital transformation is disrupting individuals and not just industries.

o Just using AI as your content is a dangerous strategy because AI lacks the unique personality in you that makes you valuable. You are not a robot and we have some time go before AI can deliver true artificial consciousness.

o Deep fakes, conversations with famous people that are fake, labor disputes and virtual influencers should be a reminder that alternatives are being sought in the fast-growing world of personal branding.

o The mobile internet needs to be your most favored friend as you plan your personal brand strategy. Leveraging social media through the mobile internet is how you reach your global audience. Connected devices, especially as they are infused with AI, will be additional opportunities to explore in the future for your brand.

o Depending on your current work role, your job may end up being put at AI risk.

o As technology adoption accelerates, artificial intelligence will be the ultimate search engine to dramatically summarize your valuable persona to potential monetizable audiences.

REFLECTION

IF YOU ASKED CHATGPT
OR ANOTHER CHATBOT, HOW
WOULD AI DESCRIBE YOU AS A
PERSONAL BRAND?

DO YOU SEE AI AS A THREAT
OR AN OPPORTUNITY FOR YOU
IN THE FUTURE?

HOW WOULD YOU DESCRIBE
ANY RECENT EXPERIENCE
WITH AI?

WHAT'S KEEPING YOU
FROM MORE AGGRESSIVELY
EMBRACING CHATGPT OR
OTHER AI CHATBOTS
IN YOUR DAILY LIFE?

CHAPTER 10

IT'S A JOURNEY, NOT A DESTINATION

> 'THE SECRET OF GETTING AHEAD IS GETTING STARTED. THE SECRET OF GETTING STARTED IS BREAKING YOUR COMPLEX OVERWHELMING TASKS INTO SMALL, MANAGEABLE TASKS AND THEN STARTING ON THE FIRST ONE.'
>
> MARK TWAIN

This chapter summarizes key ideas from this book and provides action steps that you can take to launch your new, much improved self. Overnight success is a myth. Building a personal brand involves successive steps which transport you on an amazing journey of self-discovery. Be assured, the destination will reveal itself and, like me, you will be pleasantly surprised that it exceeded what you originally dreamed of as the definition of life changing success.

RECOGNIZE EXCUSES

You might remember that in Chapter 6 I introduced the first part of the above quote from Mark Twain. To get ahead, you do indeed need to get started.

Most of us tend to be frozen in place, unfortunately often for too long, because life keeps us busily eating up what seems is too much of our time. Thoughts swirling through your mind might include:

- Work is so difficult right now and I really do not have time to focus on anything else.
- The family is growing and I need to give them more quality time.
- There is a great TV show or sports event tonight and I need to make time for it in order to relax.
- My career is going great and I don't have to worry about the future which will reveal itself as I move up the corporate ladder.
- I am miserable right now. I don't seem to have enough time for anything. No way can I squeeze in one more item.
- My family comes first. My aspirations have to come second as I need to take care of the family.
- Maybe I will invest in crypto or gold or the stock market as that will make me rich then I won't need to worry about the future.
- I have heard of this personal branding thing, but it feels like a lot of work and I am not sure of the rewards.

Given the journey I have undertaken over the last 10 years in building my own personal brand, I stress that all of the above are excuses. We all have limitations placed on us, but there are many creative options we can explore to overcome them.

The most difficult step is that first one. We tend to associate pain with venturing into the unknown. Yet your best, most monetizable self is on the other side of your comfort zone.

YOU ARE DESIGNED TO EXPLORE A WHOLE NEW WORLD

If you are a parent, think back to the excitement of your child taking their first step. We take pictures, we film it, we tell the world, about that amazing natural motion to move from point A to point B. A baby is not designed to start walking on day one of their life. It is an evolutionary journey.

That first step was preceded by a series of other developmental activities which built on each other. One of a baby's first motor skills develops at around 3 months when they are able to reach for something. Reaching gives a baby the ability to manipulate their environment and get excited by everything they touch or play with.[1]

At about 4 to 8 months of age, a baby is able to sit on their own. This new skill provides greater independence in manipulating objects and seeing in 3D orientations.[2]

After sitting, crawling typically follows at around 6 to 10 months. According to research, this is the stage when babies begin to understand depth as a cue to navigate the world safely and creates opportunities for social interactions with people around them. Because of the mechanics of crawling, most of the time the baby only sees the floor and has to stop and sit to actually see the environment, if they want a full view.[3]

The magic of that first baby step usually takes place at 13 to 15 months and is a time when the individual can navigate the environment with a full view of the scene ahead, making it easier to play with toys and even play with others. This new found freedom comes with many risks. Babies can reach for items they should not be putting in their mouth or they can touch things like electrical sockets that are dangerous. Plus, they can fall from beds or stairs as heights don't mean much at this age and they are not afraid of them.[4]

It is estimated that between 12 and 19 months a baby takes on average over 2,000 steps and falls 17 times every hour, on each occasion getting up and seeking out new pleasure possibilities.[5] The wonder of a baby courageously exploring their world after taking that first step is what you need to find once again in crafting your personal brand.

Contrary to popular belief, fear is not something we are born with. We learn to be afraid by conditioning or a negative experience.[6] There are no preconceived notions in the mind of a baby. We enter the world innocent and without fear, eager to learn more as we evolve to becoming unique human beings.

As explained earlier, pleasure and pain are the conditioning mechanisms that drive the majority of our lives. We actively seek activities that promise pleasure. We avoid taking risks because of the potential of pain.

All of us were born with that fearless baby mentality which does indeed carry risks. Confucius summarized it best, 'Our greater glory is not never falling, but in rising every time we fall.'[7] You may stumble, but you were born with the gift of continuously seeking independence. An amazing world of possibilities to really achieve your dreams is out there and with personal branding, you can take that first step to explore your full potential.

THE FIRST STEP TO LIFE CHANGING SUCCESS

I opened Chapter 1 of this book by asking whether you had Googled your name. If you have not, stop reading and do so now. The first step in personal branding is understanding how the internet defines you today.

Recall that personal branding is the deliberate crafting of your public persona including all published content created to shape it. Shaping that brand to an improved level requires a clear understanding of your skills and how they can add value to the world. Genuine self-expression, built on skills that are fine-tuned over time, is what builds successful personal brands. On the other hand, fake brands fail, and fail substantially over time.

Depending on your internet activities, Googling your name will deliver a range of results. If you are highly active on social media, it may place major focus in that area. If you have a common name, multiple pages will load and you will need to search to find out who you really are in the virtual world. If it takes a few pages to actually find you, that should not upset you. Understanding where you are, knowing what you want to become, and then putting together a plan of action are part of the process to differentiation.

A personal brand in today's digital world is more important than ever. Your name can and should be a high monetizable asset both while working in a corporation and if you decide at some point to create a full-time independent role. In the 5+ billion people connected to the global internet today, there is a valuable audience for you to reach.[8] Through this audience, you can create multiple paths to success.

A well-planned personal brand will elevate the number of people that trust you and find your thought leadership credible and valuable. Embarking on this journey will increase your curiosity and you will discover the power of continuous learning.

Once you take control of your personal narrative, it will be *you*, and not the world, that defines you. As you deliver valuable content, you will increase top-of-mind awareness, and ultimately leave your family and friends a positive documented legacy.

We are a summary of our childhood and family upbringing, education and life experiences. We evolve into unique individuals with differentiated skills. A personal brand is nothing more than a formalized approach to elevate the value and visibility of those skills to the world around you.

If you clearly define the value of your skills publicly, leveraging the new approaches introduced in this book, and then decide to decide to stay in a corporate career, you will get more promotions. While climbing that corporate ladder, other options for greater independence will reveal themselves and you will increase the number of available career paths, including full independence.

If you define a personal brand as social media in the current state, the odds that it will elevate the value of your brand right now are probably low. Social media is a technological tool. It has both negatives and positives. It can be a platform to showcase the latest party picture or a place where you introduce an innovative idea that intrigues your audience to want to learn more.

Life changing success is possible. It requires taking that first step and having the tenacity to follow it up with the next consecutive action to continuously value-add who you are.

WHAT DO YOU VALUE?

One of the greatest benefits of creating a personal brand is that it will force you to analyze who you truly are and what you are destined to become. The first and all the subsequent steps out of that realization are based on what you value, care and are passionate about as an individual.

The time that you take in defining your core principles and values will be extremely valuable to your future. Keep anything that you define as core to just the top three. My top three principles are: integrity, curiosity and leadership. Through the evolution of my personal brand, they are ingrained in every single activity, from public speaking to blogs and general posts that I believe will benefit my audience.

Your principles and values have a foundation. As you grew up, you psyche was fed by core principles. I have fond memories all the way back to kindergarten in my native country of Italy where I acted out in my first play and was amazed by the reaction of the audience. Acting was not my destiny, but marketing became my passion.

We all have both strengths and weaknesses in our personalities. Understanding clearly each of these is important in the evolution of your personal brand. Continuously work to elevate the visibility and even monetize your strengths. Accept your weaknesses and work to mitigate them with assistance from others or by learning how to improve them through research.

Go back to Chapter 2 and follow the guidelines for identifying your strengths. Learn how to translate those strengths into Unique Selling Propositions (USPs) that make you more valuable to your audience. Always remember that a successful brand requires differentiation, a reason why buying the product or idea from you is better than the competition.

Discovering what you value will be of great assistance in growing your corporate career. It will help identify areas where you are aligned and are thriving. It will also help you find gaps that potentially will lead you to explore other alternatives.

Whether you are a corporate ladder climber, someone just holding on to a job or an entrepreneur, it's the same process: identify your principles and values; from your experiences find areas that you believe need improvement; identify and work to improve your strengths; define your USPs; experiment with ideas on branding in whatever position you are in; find your autonomy, mastery and purpose to motivate yourself higher; seek mentors to give you feedback; crystallize all the inputs into a maximum of three topics for your personal brand; define your audience; embrace networking through social media to reach that audience.

FIND YOUR IDEAL COMMUNICATION CHANNEL

In this book you have met multiple individuals that have created powerful personal brands. Some of them such as Richard Branson, Elon Musk and Elvis Presley are megastars. Many others are just ordinary people that decided to differentiate themselves by elevating the value of their skills through a personal brand.

The key trait that made all these individuals successful is their ability to deliver powerful communication through various channels. The message is important, but so is the medium.

Regarding the medium, as this book has illustrated, you have a substantial number of options. I selected LinkedIn as my primary channel and X and Facebook as my secondary channels. I sporadically reinforce my visual messaging and my global reach through the use of Instagram.

None of the channels that I selected may directly apply to you. My recommendation is that you find the individuals that are either megastars or those ordinary people that share the traits of the leadership skills you want to showcase to the world. Through the internet, everything you need to find about these individuals is at your fingertips.

If you want to accelerate your journey, reach out directly to some of these key individuals and obtain their insights. Doing your homework ahead of time will allow you to focus on the most important questions you need answered to start your branding journey.

In Chapter 3, I listed 20 different social media channels from which to choose to deliver your content. Pick the channels that best fit the value you are trying to deliver through your personal brand. If it is business-to-business strategy, maybe it is LinkedIn. If it is visual as in primarily pictures, it is Instagram. For videos it might be YouTube or TikTok.

As I did, you can multi-task content across multiple channels, but always remember the Power of Three that I have mentioned several times. To keep it meaningful and minimize distractions, always select the top three and focus on these in everything you publish.

There is probably a good reason why only three medals are awarded at the Olympics. Gold should be your primary channel that will lead you to win the personal branding race. Silver and bronze are still important and in multiple ways support the gold medal of your content.

The world of technology is constantly changing. Keep an eye on new social media channels coming onto the market and evaluate whether they become one of your top three. As an example, Threads, created by Meta which also owns Facebook and Instagram, was released in 2023 to compete with X. Ask yourself the same questions I am contemplating. Should I switch from X to Threads? What are the key differences? Which of the platforms is growing? Which of the platforms is closer to the messaging I want to deliver through my personal brand? My current decision is to stay with X, but one day, I may need to re-evaluate this approach.

In summary, you have lots of choices. You need to find the ones that best fit your strategy. If unsure, do the research or reach out to people that are ahead of you in this process for advice. You are not alone on this success journey. Most of us want to help people reach their dreams. My personal philosophy is that if I help enough people on their success journey, they will pay it forward in helping others; eventually they will discover the source, and my value and audience will grow in this process.

- o Becoming successful with personal branding on social media really boils down to three simple steps:
  1. Clean up your current content that does not reflect what you aspire to be.
  2. Map out a channel strategy for marketing your brand.
  3. Measure and adjust the content based on the metrics the platforms are reporting back to you.

- o This is not a difficult process. It just needs you to take that first step in deciding that you want to take control of your future through a monetizable personal brand.

THE NOT SO SECRET FORMULA

In this book, I have outlined my specific formula that has elevated my success on my personal branding journey. The intent is to plant ideas in your mind on what is possible if you seriously want to change your life for the better.

My formula started out simply by writing blogs. It migrated to social media channels, eventually selecting my top three. It expanded to a personal website where I consolidated all my social media activities.

As I wanted to be successful in both my corporate and personal branding career, I searched and found automation tools that would allow for timely programming of content without being in front of a computer every day. Automation was critical in delivering my A game in both my corporate career and personal brand.

Productivity in the early days meant scheduling an entire week of content on a Saturday or Sunday morning and letting the computer release it at specific targeted times. With success and monetization, I added a social media manager to move to a more real time posting schedule. I spent time with the social media manager to ensure that he was matching my personal branding formula for delivering content. I trusted him, but I periodically also verified that the content was pertinent to my audience.

I adjusted the posting formula based on a 'complaint' from a senior executive in my corporate role who believed I was spending too much time on social media. Luck was on my side, as the new times selected better optimized to when my particular audience wanted to see the content.

I invested in various iterations of my personal website to make it more modern. As with everything else, I selected just three themes – retail, innovation and leadership – as the drivers for my website. The investments made in the website were with experts that could deliver a quality product with simple guidance on my part.

I also invested in a graphic designer to create templates that cut across my content and deliver a consistent professional image that speaks to the future of retail. I hired a photographer for professional headshots and standardized their usage across the internet.

The pandemic became a period of re-assessment of my social media activities and the business they generated. I adjusted the content to reflect the new realities and I pivoted to start projecting where I believed the world would go next, after the pandemic.

My formula is evolutionary. You do not need to do everything on day one. Focus on definition of your value adds, channels and the automation tools to deliver the content. Stick to your core themes and don't get distracted by the latest fads.

Consistency, consistency and, let me say it one more time, consistency is your most important formula component. In the 10 years that I have been doing this, I can count on my hands the number of times I missed delivering content. Consistency trains your audience when to expect your content and over time creates anticipation.

Incidentally, there is a reason why the opening quote for this chapter matches that in Chapter 6 where I explained my formula in more detail. As Mark Twain said, 'The secret to getting ahead is getting started' which is repeated in both chapters. But as Twain also elaborated in this chapter, 'The secret to getting started is breaking down your complex overwhelming tasks into small manageable tasks, and then starting on the first one.'[9]

Desmond Tutu put it another way, 'There is only one way to eat an elephant: one bite at a time.'[10] From both Tutu and Twain, it is the same message: don't be afraid of the big elephant that makes that first step bigger than it is. Once you take that first step and then automate the follow up, it becomes easier and the value of you as an individual dramatically increases.

PERSONAL BRANDING - MONEY VERSUS FAME

I am often asked whether my dream was to become a celebrity or create a brand that generated a lot of money. The answer is neither when I started and both as I progressed. Yet, as I write this last chapter, I am amazed and pleasantly surprised by the number of positive twists and turns my life has taken on this self-discovery journey seeking a destination.

A career setback is what started my personal brand. The objective was to define my value to the world beyond working in a corporation.

Externally, fame came first as a top 100 retail influencer over multiple years which arrived because I created and continuously value-added a personal brand. The surprise was that that same fame enhanced and grew my corporate career. Customers I met asked me industry questions and, because of research to support my personal brand, I had detailed answers. Eventually this became a regularly updated global presentation forecasting the future of retail.

As explained earlier, today we are all living in the creator economy where lots of individuals with their own brands have emerged as monetizable assets. The influencer economy is already valued at billions of dollars and annually keeps increasing.

If you deliver authenticity to your target audience, there are endless numbers of layers of influencer success that you can achieve. You do not need to be a mega celebrity or sports star to be a brand today. You can be a macro, micro or even nano influencer today and make money.

If you project valuable expertise, you can be on the speaking circuit, join boards of directors and / or offer consulting services. You can start a podcast, a webinar series, a YouTube channel, create viral content on TikTok and by growing your audience, you can monetize it all over time.

The art of self-promotion will reveal itself as you craft your personal brand. Avoiding arrogance while projecting self-confidence attracts opportunities. Your personal brand will automatically increase your executive presence in front of audiences.

The two most important words to remember in self-promotion are: confident humility. Never boast; be confident, make the other person feel important, and use subtle messaging to deliver your strongest messages.

Personal branding allowed me to retire 10 years early, monetize my brand through publishing, boards of directors and public speaking. Through the board assignment, I was recruited into new CEO / President roles with the latest arriving as I conclude this book.

I never expected to return to corporate life, but the offers and assignments became too good to resist. Reflecting on these new opportunities, the realization is that it is not just about the money.

A personal brand changed my life for the better on many levels. My expertise in my particular industry was elevated; my confidence level dramatically increased; creativity in identifying growth strategies overflowed; productivity in all aspects of my life improved; higher leadership roles were offered; and I took on the challenge to write this book.

Because of my personal brand, I am able to see more clearly opportunities around me and be selective to the ones I want to pursue. On accepting this latest corporate position, I reminded an executive friend that I am a totally different person today than I was 10 years ago when I started my personal brand.

Every day I feel energized. I spend time thinking about what I am doing and how I can improve it. I review the content going into my personal brand and I learn from it. I take the best ideas and set them aside for later usage in major presentations.

I did not let a career setback define me. I took action. I decided that I wanted to be known broadly to the world through a personal brand. I experimented with many ideas until settling on the formula in this book which I am still using today. I invested money with experts to value add the branding journey along the way by reinvesting the monetization from the brand. Now, I am going back into corporate life as a senior and confident leader with the goal of changing and value-adding an entire retail industry sector.

NEVER STOP!

Let me restate this once again as this is your biggest barrier to getting started. There is a wise Chinese proverb which states, 'A journey of a thousand miles begins with a single step.' The most difficult step you will take with personal branding is that first step beyond what you probably unconsciously are already posting on social media.

There are substantial benefits to creatively defining yourself as that is how you will actually figure out what you want to be when you grow up. The passion to do this has to come from the inside.

Think Silicon Valley or any other startup hub around the world as you approach building your personal brand. It begins with an idea on what the product should be. It takes individuals willing to take the risk and a leap of faith to actually put your money where your mouth is. It requires surrounding yourself sometimes with people smarter than you to give you guidance in those first steps. Continuously test new ideas and learn the lessons from those ideas that fail. This iterative process will crystalize your brand to what your audience will find most valuable.

A great motivational read for the personal branding journey is Apple and the creation of the iPod, the predecessor to the iPhone. The music iPod was not the first music player introduced to the market for sale. The paradigm shift was in designing a product focusing first on the customer experience and not the technology. Apple spent a lot of time studying the competition to develop unique selling propositions. Intentionally, they hid all the technology complexity and simplified the product message to just '1000 songs in your pocket'[11].

If you are successful in reaching nirvana with your personal brand, you have actually failed. Branding is a continuously iterative process that inspires you to continuously improve, not find that magic stopping point.

My key takeaway from my own personal branding journey is that I wish I had started the process much earlier in my life as the rewards have been endorphin inducing every single day. I want you to have some of that, too. It's not a difficult journey once you understand and, more importantly, customize it to your talents and even improve on my formula. The sooner you start, the greater life satisfaction you will achieve as you re-craft as necessary those steps to *your* life changing success.

WHAT DO I WANT TO BE WHEN I GROW UP?

If there is no such thing as personal branding nirvana, then what am I striving for? In the last section I will attempt to answer this question.

This book does, indeed, contain a successful formula for creating a personal brand. However, reflecting on its entirety, what it really and hopefully inspires you to do is something much more important and that is to live a life with no regrets.

My family was not wealthy. Like many others, we were immigrants to multiple foreign lands. Money did not grow on trees. The opposite, we had to work hard and we all contributed to improving our lives.

I was lucky enough to complete multiple university degrees and find my corporate calling early in my life in the retail industry. As an introvert, I chose the toughest career of direct sales as my first post college position.

As for all of us, my corporate career was not perfect. I made many mistakes, but recovered quickly. I relied too long on climbing that corporate ladder. The wakeup call I received that led to a personal brand was transformational.

The last 10 years of immersive continuous learning through a personal brand leveraging the growing technologies around me have been exceptional. Artificial Intelligence is getting ready to take it to another level.

There is no guarantee that if you decide to create a personal brand and use my formula, it will deliver similar success to mine in terms of monetary rewards. But there is a 100% guarantee that a personal brand will improve who you are, make you happier and position you for opportunities which today you cannot imagine.

In 2017, I wrote a personal article titled, *The Three Bs for a Life with No Regrets*.[12] I opened that article by saying, 'Maybe I have been luckier than most. Every day I am inspired by the potential possibilities to change the world. Every night, reminders swirl through my mind on how much I love my life.'[13]

The Three Bs of a life with no regrets are simple:

4. **BE CURIOUS** Today, if I am curious, I can ask Alexa or just Google it.

5. **BE POSITIVE** I am positive that my glass of opportunities is always half full. If you need reinforcement on the power of positive thinking, research has shown that positive people are happier, live longer and are more successful in life.[14]

6. **BE THANKFUL** On being thankful, I wrote, 'Each of us is dealt different hands in the game of life. We all experience moments of euphoria and pain. The parts in between are the normal daily grind we experience in generational sequences from youth to old age. A lesson that I learned early in my life is to be continuously thankful for any kindness, positive feedback and personal or professional milestones reached. This can be as simple as a Thank You email which to this day I still send many.'[15]

I am not sure what I want to be when I grow up, because I am still growing and I am still searching for that personal branding nirvana. We are all on a journey whose destination we cannot fully predict.

I DO KNOW, however, that my cumulative work in both my corporate career and personal branding has been extremely fulfilling. Focusing on improving myself through a personal brand is delivering on the most important reward which is leaving a lasting legacy for next generations to improve on.

The cover design of this book is the metaphor for your life. You can be chained to the dogma of a traditional life where others are in control and design it to its eventual end. Alternatively, at any age, you can break that monotonous chain and unleash your highly valuable personal brand.

You now have a successful example starting formula. So, take that first step, adapt it to your personality, stick with it and YOU too can create a life with no regrets.

SUMMARY

o We all have limitations placed on us, but there are many creative options we can explore to overcome them.

o Contrary to popular belief, fear is not something we are born with. We learn to be afraid by conditioning or a negative experience.

o A personal brand is nothing more than a formalized approach to elevate the value and visibility of your skills to the world around you.

o Whether you are a corporate ladder climber, someone just holding on to a job, or entrepreneur, it's the same process: identify your principles and values; from your experiences find areas that you believe need improvement; identify and work to improve your strengths; define your USPs; experiment with ideas on branding in whatever position you are in; find your autonomy, mastery and purpose to motivate yourself higher; seek mentors to give you feedback; crystallize all the inputs into a maximum of three topics for your personal brand; define your audience; embrace networking through social media to reach that audience.

o There are three simple steps to becoming successful with personal branding on social media: clean up your current content that does not reflect what you aspire to be; map out a channel strategy for marketing your brand; measure and adjust the content based on the metrics the platforms are reporting back to you.

o Focus on the definition of your value adds, channels where you want to showcase those values, and the automation tools to deliver the content. Stick to your core themes and don't get distracted by the latest fads.

o If you are successful in reaching nirvana with your personal brand, you have actually failed.

o It is time you took that leap to unleash your personal brand. Take that first step, stick with it and you too can create a life with no regrets.

REFLECTIONS

WHAT DO YOU WANT TO BE
WHEN YOU GROW UP?

IS YOUR GLASS HALF FULL
OR HALF EMPTY?

ARE YOU HAPPY?

WHAT FIRST STEP HAVE YOU
ALREADY TAKEN TO DEFINE
YOUR PERSONAL BRAND?

ACKNOWLEDGEMENTS

Writing this book has been an unrivalled journey of self-discovery, a journey requiring introspection and reflection learned in finding my true inner self and turning those life lessons into a public and valuable asset.

Telling the world who you really are can be scary. Advising how you, the reader, can add to valuable thought leadership to improve your life is a responsibility. As in any activity that is extraordinary, what I have found is that the support system is critical to the journey.

Unleash Your Brand is dedicated to my life time partner, Clare D'Onofrio who, from the day we met 40 plus years ago, believed and, more importantly, encouraged me to find my improved self. Early in our married life, she kept secret the financial struggles in raising our family, thereby allowing me to focus on progressing my corporate career. In times of major decisions, she has been my pillar of knowledge whose great counsel moved our lives positively forward. For my children – Monica, Michael and Nicholas – I am thankful to have you in my life and hope this book inspires you to work hard towards your own successful future identity. Always remember that what you dream about and continuously focus on, with confidence and fortitude, you will achieve.

If you truly reflect, our families, including those who preceded us, are the foundations of the personalities we are today. My father's diary that he recorded at age 18 reflected on the major difficulties of living on the front lines of World War II in Italy. My hometown, Coreno Ausonio, was on the Gustav Line, the major front where the Germans attempted to defend Italy against the advancing Allies from the south.

Starting in 1944, the family was sent to multiple concentration camps, walked many miles trying to find safety, experienced hunger, was often separated, had close relatives perish, then, post war, struggled to regain a footing in normality. I have felt honoured to publish my father's diary for our family.

Creating this book has been a reminder that I inherited the same passion for writing and leaving a legacy as my father. I am therefore thankful to him and my entire extended family in both Italy and the United States for the lessons learned and, more importantly, their continuous effort to improve the lives of the next generation.

However, family is just one major part of our personal ecosystem. I have been blessed by a tremendous number of special friends and mentors who offered valuable insights along my writing journey. Some of these were motivational groups such as Dale Carnegie that increased my optimistic view of possibilities. But the most critical to success were those mentors who, at critical decision points, offered the right advice to keep me moving forward. Five especially come to mind at this point and they are Robert Locke, my Silicon Valley innovator advisor who wrote the Foreword for this book. The second is John Smith, a wise individual and fellow executive friend whose counsel I continuously seek. Ron Assaf is the founder of the technology company, Sensormatic. I joined his company for the most amazing growth-filled, highly customer focused part of my corporate career. Mr Assaf is special because in subsequent years, he continuously tracked my career and offered praise and encouragement. My fourth mentor, George Oliver, leads the conglomerate, Johnson Controls. I appreciate George for his career guidance and, as I write these words, the opportunity to lead Sensormatic to its next successful generation. Finally, Paul Bessant is another great British friend and advisor who has provided many stages on which to share my futurist ideas including the one that officially will launch this book. Beyond these five, I am sure I have missed quite a few others that at different stages of my life stepped in to help me find the next level of inspirational success. My appreciation to all of you.

The writing process is a collaboration which goes way beyond typing words on a keyboard. Writing a book requires a success formula and the best way to discover that formula is to work with a professional. I was inspired by both the work and encouragement of my editor, Sandra Smith. The structure, flow and completion of this book is the direct result of Sandra's expert guidance.

Finally, I am appreciative of Nicholas Halliday for the excellent guidance in all the components required to publish my book. I have relied upon expertise from both Sandra and Nicholas in achieving this final product.

Along with my social media activities and my personal website (tonydonofrio.com), *Unleash Your Brand* is my inspirational legacy to my family and to all of you who have the power within to achieve extraordinary success. Creating and unleashing a personal brand is a great place to start. As Christopher Robin said, 'Always remember that you are braver than you believe, stronger that you seem, and smarter than you think.' The same positive thoughts that this book inspired remind me every day that I love my life and cannot wait for what it will reveal next.

REFERENCES

CHAPTER 1

1. Weareconvoy.com, A Brief History of Branding, https://www.weareconvoy. com/2014/01/a-brief-history-of-branding/

2. Mac History, 1984's Apple's Macintosh Commercial, https://youtu.be/VtvjbmoDx-I

3. Interbrand.com, Best Global Brands 2022, https://interbrand.com/best-brands/

4. Ibid

5. Interbrand.com, Welcome to Best Global Brands 2022, https://interbrand.com/ thinking/welcome-to-best-global-brands-2022/

6. Ibid

7. Worldpopulationreview.com, Life Expectancy by Country 2023, https:// worldpopulationreview.com/country-rankings/life-expectancy-by-country

8. Interbrand.com, Welcome to Best Global Brands 2022, https://interbrand.com/ thinking/welcome-to-best-global-brands-2022/

9. Smartinsights.com, Global Social Media Statistics Research Summary 2023, https:// www.smartinsights.com/social-media-marketing/social-media-strategy/new-global-social-media-research/

10. Ibid

11. Statista.com, Daily time spent on social networking by internet users worldwide from 2012 to 2023, https://www.statista.com/statistics/433871/daily-social-media-usage-worldwide/

12. Prweb.com, 71% of Hiring Decision-Makers Agree Social Media is Effective for Screening Applicants, https://www.prweb.com/releases/71_of_hiring_decision_makers_agree_social_media_is_effective_for_screening_applicants/prweb17467312. htm

13. Ibid

14. Ibid

15. Insidescience.org, How Much Does Earth Weigh?, https://www.insidescience.org/ video/how-much-does-earth-weigh

16. Worldometers.info, Current World Population, https://www.worldometers.info/ world-population/

17. Shortform.com, The 13 Essential Principles of Think and Grow Rich, https://www. shortform.com/blog/principles-of-think-and-grow-rich/

18. Covey, Stephen R, *The Seven Habits of Highly Effective People*, 1989, Simon and Schuster, New York

19. Definition: Trust, https://www.dictionary.com/browse/trust

20. Institutelm.com, Leadership Essentials: Building Trust, https://www.institutelm.com/learning/leadership-framework/authenticity/building-trust/leadership-essentials-building-trust.html

21. Ibid

22. QuickMBA.com, The Trusted Leader, http://www.quickmba.com/mgmt/leadership/trusted-leader/

23. Psychologytoday.com, Curiosity: The Heart of Lifelong Learning, https://www.psychologytoday.com/us/blog/the-moment-youth/201504/curiosity-the-heart-lifelong-learning

24. Futurestateengineering.com, Get Busy Living or Get Busy Dying, https://futurestateengineering.com/get-busy-living-or-get-busy-dying/

25. Zippia.com, 35+ Amazing Advertising Statistics (2023): Data + Trends, https://www.zippia.com/advice/advertising-statistics/

26. Ibid

27. Ibid

28. Ibid

29. Domo.com, Data Never Sleeps 10.0, https://www.domo.com/data-never-sleeps

30. Ibid

31. Wikipedia.org, Benjamin Franklin, https://en.wikipedia.org/wiki/Benjamin_Franklin

32. Graciousquotes.com, 79 Inspiring Gary Vaynerchuk Quotes (Hustling), https://graciousquotes.com/gary-vee-quotes/

CHAPTER 2

1. What do you stand for? An Exercise to Discover your Values https://www.fearlessculture.design/blog-posts/what-do-you-stand-for-an-exercise-to-discover-your-values

2. What do you stand for, Really? https://www.fearlessculture.design/blog-posts/what-do-you-stand-for-really

3. Motivated Implicit Theories of Personality: My Weaknesses Will Go Away, but My Strengths are Here to Stay, April 2016 https://www.researchgate.net/publication/298733083_Motivated_Implicit_Theories_of_Personality_My_Weaknesses_Will_Go_Away_but_My_Strengths_Are_Here_to_Stay

4. What is Negativity Bias and How can it be Overcome? December 2019 https://positivepsychology.com/3-steps-negativity-bias/

5. How to Play to Your Strengths, Harvard Business Review, January 2005 https://hbr.org/2005/01/how-to-play-to-your-strengths

6. Work on Your Strengths, Not Your Weaknesses, May 2019 https://zapier.com/blog/how-to-find-your-strengths/

7. 5 Ways to Identify Your Strengths and What you are Good At, February 2023 https://www.trackinghappiness.com/how-to-identify-your-strengths/

8. Ibid

9. What is a Unique Selling Proposition? October 2022 https://www.shopify.com/blog/unique-selling-proposition

10. Definition: Proposition, https://www.vocabulary.com/dictionary/proposition

11. How to Build Your Personal Brand at Work, Harvard Business Review, September 2022 https://hbr.org/2022/09/how-to-build-your-personal-brand-at-work

12. 20 Eye-Opening Statistics About the State of Career Changes in 2023, March 2023 https://goremotely.net/blog/career-change-statistics/

13. Pink's Autonomy, Mastery and Purpose Framework, Mind Tools, https://www.mindtools.com/asmdp60/pinks-autonomy-mastery-and-purpose-framework

14. Ibid

15. The Literature Network, A Tale of Two Cities by Charles Dickens, Chapter 1, https://www.online-literature.com/dickens/twocities/1/

16. How Many New Businesses are Started Each Year. Data Reveals the Answer, Commerce Institute https://www.commerceinstitute.com/new-businesses-started-every-year/

17. Regrets of the Dying, Bronnie Ware, https://bronnieware.com/blog/regrets-of-the-dying/

18. Covey, SR The Seven Habits of Highly Effective People, 1989, Simon and Schuster, New York

19. Ibid

20. Regrets of the Dying, Bronnie Ware, https://bronnieware.com/blog/regrets-of-the-dying/

CHAPTER 3

1. Did you know? Free Working Tricks, https://youtu.be/u06BXgWbGvA

2. Frequency of using selected news sources among Generation Z in the United States as of August 2022, Statista, https://www.statista.com/statistics/1124119/gen-z-news-consumption-us/

3. On Being Social Beings, Oberlin College for Convergence, 2021, https://www.oberlin.edu/oberlin-center-convergence/oberlin-center-convergence/learning-communities/on-being-social-beings

4. Why do people use social media? Oberlo, https://www.oberlo.com/statistics/why-do-people-use-social-media

5. Day of Eight Billion, United Nations, https://www.un.org/en/dayof8billion

6. Digital 2023: Global Overview Report, Datareportal.com, https://datareportal.com/reports/digital-2023-global-overview-report

7. Ibid

8. Digital 2023 Deep-Dive: How Much Time Do we Spend on Social Media?, Datareportal.com, https://datareportal.com/reports/digital-2023-deep-dive-time-spent-on-social-media

9. Ibid

10. Ibid

11. Ibid

12. The 2023 Global Social Media Trends Report, HubSpot and Brandwatch, https://offers.hubspot.com/social-media-trends-report

13. Ibid

14. Ibid

15. 120 Social Media Sites You Need to Know in 2023, Influencer Marketing Hub, December 2022 128 Social Media Sites You Need to Know in 2023 (influencermarketinghub.com)

16. 21 Top Social Media Sites to Consider for Your Brand in 2023, Buffer, March 2023 Top Social Media Sites to Consider for Your Brand in 2023 (buffer.com)

17. Social Media Platform Comparison, SEO Design Chicago, https://seodesignchicago.com/marketing/social-media-platform-comparison/

18. Ibid

19. Ibid

20. Ibid

21. Ibid

22. Ibid

23. With the exodus of young users from Facebook, advertisers are revising their pitch. Socialsamosa.com, January 2023 https://www.socialsamosa.com/2023/01/facebook-advertisers-strategy-2023/

24. What happens in an internet minute, The Infographic Show, March 2023 https://youtu.be/KchfTwp0PpM

25. Social Media Platform Comparison, SEO Design Chicago, https://seodesignchicago.com/marketing/social-media-platform-comparison/

26. Ibid

27. 5 Reasons why video is more effective than the written word, IdeaRocketAutomation.com, September 2022 https://idearocketanimation.com/17385-reasons-video-effective-text/

28. Social Media Platform Comparison, SEO Design Chicago, https://seodesignchicago.com/marketing/social-media-platform-comparison/

29. Ibid

CHAPTER 4

1. Famous Failures, Steemit.com, https://steemit.com/life/@kalco10/famous-failures

2. 9 Famous Success Through Failure Stories to Get you Motivated, Visualistan.com, April 23, 2016 https://www.visualistan.com/2016/04/9-famous-success-trough-failure-stories.html

3. University of Houston College of Global Hospitality Leadership, Colonel Harland Sanders, https://www.uh.edu/hilton-college/About/Hospitality-Industry-Hall-of-Honor/Inductees/Colonel-Harland-Sanders%20/

4. 15 Highly Successful People who Failed Before Succeeding, Lifehack.org, September 26, 2022 https://www.lifehack.org/articles/productivity/15-highly-successful-people-who-failed-their-way-success.html

5. 10 Famous Failures That'll Inspire You to Try One More Time, Oberlo.com, September 4, 2018 https://www.oberlo.com/blog/famous-failures

6. Mark Twain Quotes, Goodreads.com, https://www.goodreads.com/quotes/2528-keep-away-from-people-who-try-to-belittle-your-ambitions

7. Richard Branson, Forbes https://www.forbes.com/profile/richard-branson/

8. Richard Branson, Twitter Profile https://twitter.com/richardbranson

9. Richard Branson, Biography.com, November 2, 2021 https://www.biography.com/business-leaders/richard-branson

10. Ibid

11. Ibid

12. Virgin Group, About Us, https://www.virgin.com/about-virgin/virgin-group

13. Richard Branson, Biography.com, November 2, 2021 https://www.biography.com/business-leaders/richard-branson

14. Ibid

15. Ibid

16. 13 Brilliant and Outlandish Marketing Stunts Used by Richard Branson, AmericanExpress.com, October 20, 2014 https://www.americanexpress.com/en-us/business/trends-and-insights/articles/14-brilliant-outlandish-stunts-richard-branson-used-market-virgin/

17. Virgin Tycoon is Knighted, BBC News, March 30, 2000 http://news.bbc.co.uk/2/hi/uk_news/695511.stm

18. Sir Richard Branson net worth – all you need to know the entrepreneur and how he makes his money, Goodto.com, December 7, 2022 https://www.goodto.com/entertainment/richard-branson-net-worth-how-makes-his-money

19. Richard Branson's Story, Virgin.com, https://www.virgin.com/branson-family/richard-branson

20. Top 10 Most Followed Account on Linkedin, BusinessConnectIndia.com, June 12, 2023 https://businessconnectindia.in/top-10-most-followed-account-on-linkedin/

21. Richard Branson LinkedIn Profile, June 14, 2023 https://www.LinkedIn.com/in/rbranson/

22. List of Dyslexic Achievers, dyslexia.com, https://www.dyslexia.com/about-dyslexia/dyslexic-achievers/all-achievers/

23. Richard Branson: The Poster Boy of Personal Branding, Connected.co, July 10, 2017 https://www.connectedwomen.co/magazine/richard-branson-the-poster-boy-of-personal-branding/

24. Ibid

25. Richard Branson: On Branding, SomeoneInLondon.com, https://someoneinlondon.com/updates/richard-branson-on-branding

26. Elon Musk, Forbes Profile https://www.forbes.com/profile/elon-musk/?sh=3830cf507999

27. Elon Musk, Britannica.com, June 16, 2023 https://www.britannica.com/biography/Elon-Musk

28. Who is Elon Musk?, Investopedia.com, October 28, 2022 https://www.investopedia.com/articles/personal-finance/061015/how-elon-musk-became-elon-musk.asp#citation-54

29. Ibid

30. Ibid

31. Ibid

32. Ibid

33. Ibid

34. Ibid

35. Ibid

36. How does Elon Musk Make Money?, FourweekMBA.com, May 22, 2023 https://fourweekmba.com/elon-musk-companies/

37. How Many Teslas Have Been Sold?, Licarco.com, April 3, 2023 https://www.licarco.com/news/how-many-tesla-cars-have-been-sold

38. Elon Musk says he's an unrelenting optimistic. Warren Buffett made a similar point about Tesla chief's vision and drive, Business Insider, May 23, 2023 https://markets.businessinsider.com/news/stocks/elon-musk-warren-buffett-tesla-spacex-munger-optimism-insurance-billionaires-2023-5

39. Ibid

40. Elon Musk Twitter Profile https://twitter.com/elonmusk

41. 90+ Inspiring Dalai Lama Quotes to Change your Outlook on Life, declutterthemind.com, December 22, 2020 https://declutterthemind.com/blog/dalai-lama-quotes/

42. Steve Jobs' 2005 Stanford Commencement Address (with intro by President John Hennessy), YouTube.com https://youtu.be/Hd_ptbiPoXM

43. Why is Elvis called "the King of Rock 'n' Roll"? Britannica.com, https://www.britannica.com/story/why-is-elvis-called-the-king-of-rock-n-roll

44. Who were Elvis' Parents Vernon + Gladys Presley Encouraged the icon to pursue music, WideOpenCountry.com, February 7, 2023 https://www.wideopencountry.com/elvis-presley-parents/

45. Elvis Presley Biography & Accomplishments, study.com, https://study.com/learn/lesson/elvis-presley-biography-early-life-accomplishments-music.html

46. Ibid

47. Ibid

48. Ibid

49. Ibid

50. Ibid

51. Ibid

52. Elvis Presley Achievements, Graceland.com, https://www.graceland.com/achievements

53. Ibid

54. This Day in History – 1977 Elvis Presley Dies, History.com, https://www.history.com/this-day-in-history/elvis-presley-dies

55. Elvis Movie Released in 2022, https://www.rottentomatoes.com/m/elvis

56. Why is Elvis Called "the King of Rock 'n' Roll"? Britannica.com, https://www.britannica.com/story/why-is-elvis-called-the-king-of-rock-n-roll

57. Parable: The Emperor Has No Clothes, Medium.com, April 16, 2019 https://medium.com/@mattimore/parable-the-emperor-has-no-clothes-ace63fef6eb8

CHAPTER 5

1. Where are you headed: Greatness or Mediocrity?, Forbes, May 10, 2012 https://www.forbes.com/sites/barbarastanny/2012/05/10/where-are-you-headed-greatness-or-mediocrity/

2. Change: The Power of Leverage, Tony Robbins https://www.tonyrobbins.com/resources/pdfs/The-Power-of-Leverage.pdf

3. Ibid

4. Gary Vee Net Worth: Income, Investments and Career, abcactionnews.com, March 17, 2023, https://www.abcactionnews.com/sponsor-generated-content/gary-vee-net-worth#

5. Ibid

6. Ibid

7. Ibid

8. Ibid

9. Ibid

10. Gary Vaynerchuk LinkedIn Profile, https://www.LinkedIn.com/in/garyvaynerchuk/

11. Gary Vee Net Worth: Income, Investments and Career, abcactionnews.com, March 17, 2023, https://www.abcactionnews.com/sponsor-generated-content/gary-vee-net-worth#

12. Neil Patel Profile, NeilPatel.com, https://neilpatel.com/about/

13. Ibid

14. Ibid

15. Ibid

16. Ibid

17. Who is Neil Patel?, lxahub.com, March 20, 2023 https://www.lxahub.com/stories/neil-patel

18. Neil Patel LinkedIn Profile, https://www.LinkedIn.com/in/neilkpatel/

19. Ibid

20. Carol Tice, Seattle Freelance Writer, caroltice.com, https://www.caroltice.com/about/

21. Ibid

22. Ibid

23. Ibid

24. From Fired Journalist to Six-Figure Freelancer: Carol Tice on the Single, Most Powerful Force that Moves Your Writing Forward, thebarefootwriter.com, https://www.thebarefootwriter.com/writer-success-stories/fired-journalist-six-figure-freelancer-carol-tice-single-powerful-force-moves-writing-business-forward

25. Ibid

26. Ibid

27. Ibid

28. Carol Tice's Branding Success Story (and How you can do the Same), speakersinstitute.com, December 9, 2020, https://www.speakersinstitute.com/carol-tices-branding-success-story-and-how-you-can-do-the-same/

29. Carol Tice, Seattle Freelance Writer, caroltice.com, https://www.caroltice.com/about/

30. Carol Tice's Branding Success Story (and How you can do the Same), speakersinstitute.com, December 9, 2020, https://www.speakersinstitute.com/carol-tices-branding-success-story-and-how-you-can-do-the-same/

31. Carol Tice, Thinkers360.com, https://www.thinkers360.com/tl/profiles/view/9729

32. My Story: Battling Self-Doubt to Blogging Success, AdamEnfroy.com, https://www.adamenfroy.com/my-story

33. Ibid

34. Ibid

35. Ibid

36. Ibid

37. Ibid

38. Ibid

39. Ibid

40. Ibid

41. Ibid

42. Ibid

43. Adam Enfroy LinkedIn Profile https://www.LinkedIn.com/in/adamenfroy/

44. Adam Enfroy's Net Worth: How Does He Make $350,000 per Month as a Full-Time Blogger?, blog.symalite.com, December 13, 2022 https://blog.symalite.com/adam-enfroy/

45. 100 Top Micro-Influencers to Follow in 2023, Amraandelma.com, https://www.amraandelma.com/top-micro-influencers/

46. Ibid

47. Ibid

48. The Closet Crush, https://theclosetcrush.com/

49. 100 Top Micro-Influencers to Follow in 2023, Amraandelma.com, https://www.amraandelma.com/top-micro-influencers/

50. Gritty Pretty, https://grittypretty.com.au/magazine/

51. 100 Top Micro-Influencers to Follow in 2023, Amraandelma.com, https://www.amraandelma.com/top-micro-influencers/

52. Fran Newman Young Blog, https://frannewmanyoung.com/

53. 100 Top Micro-Influencers to Follow in 2023, Amraandelma.com, https://www.amraandelma.com/top-micro-influencers/

54. Cotter Crunch Website, https://www.cottercrunch.com/

55. 100 Top Micro-Influencers to Follow in 2023, Amraandelma.com, https://www.amraandelma.com/top-micro-influencers/

56. Technical Dost YouTube Channel, https://www.youtube.com/@TechnicalDost

57. 50 Top Nano Influencers in 2023, Amraandelma.com, https://www.amraandelma.com/top-nano-influencers/

58. Ibid

59. Petal and Seeds Instagram Site, https://www.instagram.com/petalsandseeds/

60. Chantelle Coustol YouTube Channel, https://www.youtube.com/@ chantellecoustol3091

61. 50 Top Nano Influencers in 2023, Amraandelma.com, https://www.amraandelma. com/top-nano-influencers/

CHAPTER 6

1. The Next Logical Step, tonydonofrio.com, August 5, 2012 https://tonydonofrio.com/ blog/technology/the-next-logical-step.html

2. Ibid

3. Ibid

4. 30+ YouTube Statistics and Facts (Current Year), comparitech.com, June 13, 2023 https://www.comparitech.com/tv-streaming/youtube-statistics/

5. Digital 2023: Global Overview Report, Datareportal.com, https://datareportal.com/ reports/digital-2023-global-overview-report

6. Definition: Hypothesis, OxfordLearnersdictionary.com, https://www. oxfordlearnersdictionaries.com/us/definition/english/hypothesis?q=hypothesis

7. Ralph Waldo Emerson Quotes, Goodreads.com, https://www.goodreads.com/author/ quotes/12080.Ralph_Waldo_Emerson

8. Flipboard, flipboard.com, https://flipboard.com/

9. Social Bee, https://socialbee.com/

10. What Really are the Best Times to Post on Social Media in 2023?, Neal Schaffer, March 28, 2023 https://nealschaffer.com/best-times-to-post-on-social-media/

11. Ibid

12. Social Media Statistics 2023: Top Networks by the Numbers, dustinstout.com, https:// dustinstout.com/social-media-statistics/

13. Tony D'Onofrio Personal Website, https://tonydonofrio.com/

14. The greatest glory in living is not in falling, but in rising every time we fall. NelsonMandela.co.za, https://nelsonmandelasquare.co.za/the-greatest-glory-in-living-is-not-in-falling-but-in-rising-every-time-we-fall/

CHAPTER 7

1. The Creator Economy Could Approach Half-a-Trillion dollars by 2027, Goldman Sachs 19 April 2023 https://www.goldmansachs.com/intelligence/pages/the-creator-economy-could-approach-half-a-trillion-dollars-by-2027.html

2. What is an Influencer? – Social Media Influencers Defined (updated 2023), Influencer Marketing Hub, 14 March 2023 https://influencermarketinghub.com/what-is-an-influencer/

3. Ibid

4. What is Influencer Marketing?, McKinsey & Company, April 10, 2023 https://www.mckinsey.com/featured-insights/mckinsey-explainers/what-is-influencer-marketing

5. Ibid

6. Ibid

7. Word-of-Mouth Marketing: Stats and Trends for 2023, lxahub.com, April 22, 2022 https://www.lxahub.com/stories/word-of-mouth-marketing-stats-and-trends-for-2023

8. The Click Farm, Kinfolk.com Issue 37, https://www.kinfolk.com/the-click-farm/

9. What is Influencer Marketing?, McKinsey & Company, April 10, 2023 https://www.mckinsey.com/featured-insights/mckinsey-explainers/what-is-influencer-marketing

10. The Top 100 Social Media Influencers Worldwide, Search Engine Journal, January 10, 2023 https://www.searchenginejournal.com/top-social-media-influencers/475776/#close

11. Narendra Modi, Elon Musk, Among 10 Most Followed on Twitter, India Economic Times, May 24, 2023 https://economictimes.indiatimes.com/news/web-stories/narendra-modi-elon-musk-among-10-most-followed-people-on-twitter/slideshow/100477826.cms

12. Top 10 Most Followed Account on Linkedin, Business Connect India, April 21, 2023 https://businessconnectindia.in/top-10-most-followed-account-on-linkedin/

13. The 20 Most Followed Celebrities on Instagram in the World, The Siasat Daily, April 21, 2023 https://www.siasat.com/top-20-most-followed-celebrities-on-instagram-in-the-world-2573484/

14. 10 Most Followed Person on Facebook Updated List (2023), Infostor March 21, 2023 https://www.infostor.com/social-media/most-followed-person-on-facebook-top-celebrities-to-follow/

15. The Ten Most Subscribed YouTube Channels in the World, Lifestyle Asia, May 26, 2023 https://www.lifestyleasia.com/hk/entertainment/most-subscribed-youtube-channels-in-the-world/

16. The Most Followed TikTok Accounts in 2023, Evening Standard, April 20, 2023 https://www.standard.co.uk/news/world/most-followed-tiktok-accounts-2023-who-person-khaby-lame-b1009038.html

17. Apparently Beyonce's social media posts are worth more than a million bucks, Time Magazine, April 4, 2017 What Are Beyonce's Social Media Posts Worth? | Time

18. The Most Followed TikTok Accounts in 2023, Evening Standard, April 20, 2023 https://www.standard.co.uk/news/world/most-followed-tiktok-accounts-2023-who-person-khaby-lame-b1009038.html

19. Different types of influencers: Mega, Macro, Micro, & Nano, Amire.com, July 30, 2020 https://www.amire.com.au/blog/different-types-of-influencers

20. Ibid

21. Ibid

22. Ibid

23. Micro, Macro, Nano, Mega Influencers: Which will help you grow?, Websitebuilderexpert.com, November 9, 2022 https://www.websitebuilderexpert.com/grow-online/micro-macro-nano-mega-influencers/

24. How much do influences make in 2023? Hootsuite, October 3, 2022 https://blog.hootsuite.com/how-much-do-influencers-make/

25. Ralph Waldo Emerson Quotes, Goodreads https://www.goodreads.com/quotes/24142-life-is-a-journey-not-a-destination

26. The most important consulting industry statistics in 2023, gitnux.com, May 20, 2023 https://blog.gitnux.com/consulting-industry-statistics/

27. How much board of directors members get paid and what they do, Investopedia.com, October 22, 2022 https://www.investopedia.com/articles/wealth-management/040416/retired-execs-what-do-corporate-boards-pay.asp

28. Do the thing you fear most and the death of fear is certain, Brainyquotes.com, https://www.brainyquote.com/quotes/mark_twain_141714

29. Personal Branding: How to build your brand and make some serious money fast, Founderjar.com, December 6, 2022 https://www.founderjar.com/personal-branding/

30. Gary Vaynerchuk LinkedIn Profile https://www.LinkedIn.com/in/garyvaynerchuk/

31. Gary Vaynerchuk: Building Personal Brand Within the Social Media Landscape, YouTube https://youtu.be/EhqZ0RU95d4

CHAPTER 8

1. Five Lifetime Thanksgiving Leadership Lessons for Success, TonyDonofrio.com, November 29, 2015 https://tonydonofrio.com/blog/leadership/five-lifetime-thanksgiving-leadership-lessons-for-success.html

2. Ibid

3. Golda Meir quote, Brainyquote.com https://www.brainyquote.com/quotes/golda_meir_162893

4. Definition: Confidence, Dictionary.com, https://www.dictionary.com/browse/confidence

5. Origin of the word confidence, Online Etymology Dictionary, https://www.etymonline.com/word/confidence

6. The Dangers of Arrogance, Long Island Psychology, liphycologist.com, August 21, 2021 https://lipsychologist.com/the-dangers-of-arrogance/

7. What is Self-Confidence?, University of South Florida, usf.edu, https://www.usf.edu/student-affairs/counseling-center/top-concerns/what-is-self-confidence.aspx

8. Why Self-Confidence is More Important than You Think, Psychology Today, September 20, 2018, https://www.psychologytoday.com/us/blog/shyness-is-nice/201809/why-self-confidence-is-more-important-you-think

9. Ibid

10. The Science of Having More Confidence, HoffeldGroup.com, https://www.hoffeldgroup.com/the-science-of-having-more-confidence/

11. What is Executive Presence? The Leadership Quality No One Told You About, emeritus.org, July 15, 2022, https://emeritus.org/blog/what-is-executive-presence/

12. Level 5 Leadership: The Triumph of Humility and Fierce Resolve, *Harvard Business Review*, January 1, 2001, https://hbr.org/2001/01/level-5-leadership-the-triumph-of-humility-and-fierce-resolve-2

13. Ibid

14. Ibid

15. Ibid

16. 35+ Amazing Advertising Statistics (2023): Data + Trends, zippia.com, June 13, 2023 https://www.zippia.com/advice/advertising-statistics/

17. Ibid

18. Ibid

19. Bragging vs Self-Promotion, powerwoe.com, https://www.powerwoe.com/bragging-vs-self-promotion/

20. Importance of Social Media Images for Digital Marketing – 7 Tips for Amazing Pictures!, socialchamp.io, March 17, 2021, https://www.socialchamp.io/blog/social-media-images-ideas

21. Retail Technology Series: AI's Impact on Retail Through 2029, YouTube.com, Conversations on Retail, June 27, 2023, https://youtu.be/9aGemTVUObo

22. Is self-promotion evaluated more positively if it is accurate? Reexamining the role of accuracy and modesty on the perception of self-promotion, tandfonline.com, April 25, 2018, https://www.tandfonline.com/doi/figure/10.1080/15298868.2018.1465846

23. Savvy Self-Promotion, Harvard Business Review, May-June 2020, https://hbr.org/2021/05/savvy-self-promotion

24. Ibid

25. Ibid

26. 3 Effective Self-Promotion Strategies Backed by Science, recruiter.com, https://www.recruiter.com/recruiting/3-effective-self-promotion-strategies-backed-by-science/

27. Ibid

28. Marcus Tullius Cicero Quote, brainyquote.com, https://www.brainyquote.com/quotes/marcus_tullius_cicero_134884

29. PT Barnum Biography, biography.com, https://www.biography.com/business-leaders/pt-barnum

CHAPTER 9

1. Buzzing Past the Hype of Digital Transformation, July 15, 2023, tonydonofrio.com, https://tonydonofrio.com/blog/technology/the-rise-of-the-faster-smarter-machines-continues.html

2. Take a deep look at the history of digital transformation, May 8, 2022, magenest.com, https://magenest.com/en/history-of-digital-transformation/

3. 33 incredible digital transformation statistics (2023): Need to know facts on the future of business, November 14, 2022, zippia.com, https://www.zippia.com/advice/digital-transformation-statistics/

4. Ibid

5. Long Waves: The History of Innovation Cycles, June 30, 2021, Visualcapitalist.com, https://www.visualcapitalist.com/the-history-of-innovation-cycles/

6. Ibid

7. Ibid

8. Ibid

9. Ibid

10. Buzzing Past the Hype of Digital Transformation, July 15, 2023, tonydonofrio.com, https://tonydonofrio.com/blog/technology/the-rise-of-the-faster-smarter-machines-continues.html

11. The Mobile Economy 2023, gsma.com, https://www.gsma.com/mobileeconomy/wp-content/uploads/2023/03/270223-The-Mobile-Economy-2023.pdf

12. Buzzing Past the Hype of Digital Transformation, July 15, 2023, tonydonofrio.com, https://tonydonofrio.com/blog/technology/the-rise-of-the-faster-smarter-machines-continues.html

13. Ibid

14. ChatGPT Statistics 2023, tooltester.com, July 19, 2023, https://www.tooltester.com/en/blog/chatgpt-statistics/

15. Threads Shoots Past One Million Mark at Lightning Speed, July 7, 2023, statista.com, https://www.statista.com/chart/29174/time-to-one-million-users/

16. AI query engines including ChatGPT https://poe.com/

17. Ibid

18. The Deepfake Dangers Ahead, *The Wall Street Journal*, February 23, 2023, https://www.wsj.com/articles/the-deepfake-dangers-ahead-b08e4ecf

19. Character.ai website https://beta.character.ai/

20. Why Are Hollywood Actors on Strike? CBS News, July 19, 2023 https://www.cbsnews.com/news/sag-aftra-strike-hollywood-union-actors/

21. How to protect your images from AI art generators, makeuseof.com, February 8, 2023, https://www.makeuseof.com/protect-images-from-ai-art-generators/

22. It's Molly M-AI! Meet the AI influencers already making millions from mega deals with fashion giants - could you tell they don't exist? The US Sun, July 30, 2023, https://www.the-sun.com/tech/8725778/ai-influencers-fashion-deals/

23. Ibid

24. Ibid

25. The AI Disruptive Future of Retail, tonydonofrio.com, June 25, 2023, https://tonydonofrio.com/blog/retail/the-ai-disruptive-future-of-retail.html

26. Ibid

27. Ibid

28. These are the jobs most likely to be lost – and created – because of AI, World Economic Forum, May 4, 2023 https://www.weforum.org/agenda/2023/05/jobs-lost-created-ai-gpt/

29. Ibid

30. What can you tell me about the online personal brand of Tony D'Onofrio? AI question asked on https://poe.com/

CHAPTER 10

1. On a Baby's First Steps, June 3, 2019, psychologytoday.com, https://www.psychologytoday.com/us/blog/the-baby-scientist/201906/babys-first-steps

2. Ibid

3. Ibid

4. Ibid

5. Ibid

6. How we Learn to be Afraid, October 12, 2020, psychologytoday.com, https://www.psychologytoday.com/us/blog/the-baby-scientist/202010/how-we-learn-be-afraid

7. Confucius quote, brainyquote.com, https://www.brainyquote.com/quotes/confucius_101164

8. Digital 2023: Global Overview Report, Datareportal.com, https://datareportal.com/reports/digital-2023-global-overview-report

9. Mark Twain Quote, https://www.goodreads.com/quotes/219455-the-secret-of-getting-ahead-is-getting-started-the-secret

10. The only way to eat an elephant, psychologytoday.com, April 24, 2018, https://www.psychologytoday.com/us/blog/mindfully-present-fully-alive/201804/the-only-way-to-eat-an-elephant

11. Innovation Lessons from Apple and Steve Jobs: Story of the iPod, April 24, 2014, ignitionframework.com, https://www.ignitionframework.com/innovation-lessons-steve-jobs-apple-story-ipod/

12. The Three Be's for a Life with No Regrets, tonydonofrio.com, August 5, 2017, https://tonydonofrio.com/blog/leadership/the-three-be-s-for-a-life-with-no-regrets.html

13. Ibid

14. 5 Scientific Studies that Prove the Power of Positive Thinking, LinkedIn.com, March 22, 2016, https://www.LinkedIn.com/pulse/5-scientific-studies-prove-power-positive-thinking-mark-guidi/

15. The Three Be's for a Life with No Regrets, tonydonofrio.com, August 5, 2017, https://tonydonofrio.com/blog/leadership/the-three-be-s-for-a-life-with-no-regrets.html

Tony D'Onofrio

AUTHOR

After growing up in a small mountain town of central Italy, Tony D'Onofrio moved with his family to the US. Although initially struggling to deal with the culture shock, he went on to embrace the American Dream, gaining a BA in Pre-Law at Case Western Reserve University which was followed by a Marketing MBA from Cleveland State University, a springboard to a highly successful career.

Tony is CEO of the advisory group TD Insights where globally he is recognized as a social media influencer in retail, security and emerging technologies. Over multiple years including 2023, he has been listed as a top 100 Global Retail Influencer, publishes regularly on multiple platforms, has a long running weekly podcast, a webinar series on the future of retail technologies, a growing YouTube channel, and continues to share futurist retail trends through keynote presentations on many global stages.

Tony's executive experience includes positions at retail information and security technology corporations. He has mentored Silicon Valley startup companies, held multiple board roles in next generation technologies, and regularly engages with the world's largest retailers. In 2023 he was appointed President of Sensormatic, the leading global retail solutions portfolio of Johnson Controls.

With a presence and large following across multiple social media platforms, Tony's understanding of the importance of creating a personal brand has led to not only recognition as a global retail influencer, but becoming an expert in creating powerful brands that elevate the value of corporate careers while simultaneously creating multiple paths to fulfilling personal and financial life-changing success.

Unleash Your Brand is Tony's first book.

UNLEASH YOUR BRAND
DISCOVER THE KEY TO MONETIZING YOUR OWN PERSONAL BRAND

BY TONY D'ONOFRIO

Published by T.D. Insights

2024 © Tony D'Onofrio

Cover and text design and formatting:
Nicholas Halliday · HallidayBooks.com
Editer: Sandra Smith · TheCurrentMrsSmith.co.uk

This edition published, 2024
First published in hardback, 2023

TONY D'ONOFRIO INSIGHTS
TONYDONOFRIO.COM